Queen Victoria with her great-grandchildren Prince Edward (at the back), Prince Albert (left) and Princess Mary of York at Balmoral in September 1898.

QUEEN VICTORIA'S FAMILY

A Century of Photographs
1840–1940

CHARLOTTE ZEEPVAT

SUTTON PUBLISHING

First published in 2001 by
Sutton Publishing Limited · Phoenix Mill
Thrupp · Stroud · Gloucestershire · GL5 2BU

British Library Cataloguing in Publication Data
A catalogue record for this book is available from the British Library

ISBN 0 7509 2687 2

Typeset in 13/18pt Bembo.
Typesetting and origination by
Sutton Publishing Limited.
Printed in Great Britain by
J.H. Haynes & Co. Ltd, Sparkford, England.

Contents

Namesakes: the Queen's eldest daughter Victoria, 'Vicky', Princess Royal and Crown Princess of Prussia, with her daughter Victoria in about 1870.

Introduction

The beginning of Queen Victoria's reign coincided almost exactly with the first tentative steps into the world of photography. In 1837, the year of the Queen's accession, Louis Daguerre published details of his photographic process, which could fix an image on a chemically sensitised metal plate. There were other pioneers, other processes, but this was the first which was practicable. The twenty-minute exposure time made portraiture an impossibility, though, it took three more years to refine both chemicals and lenses sufficiently for that. The daguerreotype did not produce a negative, so each image was unique. The Queen is said to have been shown her first daguerreotype on the day she proposed to Prince Albert, 15 October 1839. She and the Prince bought some imported daguerreotypes in the spring of 1840; they were impressed but there was still nothing personal about the photograph – it was just a clever novelty. The first portrait studio in England using the daguerreotype process was opened by Richard Beard in London in 1841, but it was not until 1842 that a member of the royal family – Prince Albert – first sat in front of a camera, in William Constable's Brighton studio. The result must have pleased him: a few weeks later he called at Beard's studio in London and had six portraits made.

The genie was out of the bottle and royal photography developed apace. In 1841 William Henry Fox Talbot had patented the Calotype process, which used chemically treated paper to produce a paper negative – making it possible for multiple copies to be made from a single exposure. One of the miniature painters patronised by the Queen, Henry Collen, was the first to obtain a licence to use Fox Talbot's process and in 1844 or '45 he took the first known photograph of the Queen. Her eldest daughter Victoria, 'Vicky', the Princess Royal, then just four or five years old, shared the sitting, leaning against her mother's lap with her doll in her arms. In 1847 William Kilburn was invited to take daguerreotypes of the whole royal family – they sat in the greenhouse at Buckingham Palace where the light was good. Kilburn was appointed 'Photographist to Her Majesty and His Royal Highness Prince Albert' and would be given more sittings, but as the 1840s gave way to the 1850s others were coming to share the honour. Enthusiastic amateurs like the Prince's librarian Dr Becker and his equerry Captain Dudley de Ros took a number of photographs of the royal family in the 1850s: in 1853 Becker was a founder member of the Photographic Society and the Queen and the Prince became enthusiastic patrons, taking an interest in the process of photography as well as the results. They were said to have been skilful photographers themselves, though none of their work has survived.

These early royal photographs were, in a curious way, less formal than those that came later. Exposure times were long, but the family simply faced the camera as they were, in their everyday clothes, for their own interest and amusement. Many of the photographers were already well known to them and there was no thought that the public might see the results. Paper photographs were arranged carefully in albums; the couple enjoyed making these up and were pleased to show them to members of the Household, but that was all. The change came as the cost of photography dropped and the technology improved. In the mid-1850s another Frenchman, André Disderi, invented a way of taking several different exposures on a single plate. The end product was a sheet of small photographs, each measuring about 3½ by 2¼ inches (90 by 57mm), which could be separated and mounted on a card about the size of a standard visiting card – the carte-de-visite photograph. There had already been small card-mounted photographs but Disderi was the first to achieve commercial success with the idea. Cartes were cheap to produce and by the late 1850s were all the rage. Cartes of the French royal family proved popular and the American photographer John Jabez Mayall, who had already been granted a number of sittings with the Queen and Prince Albert and their children, was the first to seize the opportunity in this country. He requested permission to take cartes of the royal family and was allowed sittings in May and July 1860. His first collection was published, with permission, in August 1860 under the title *Royal Album*: it was a runaway success.

Photography has become so much part of our lives that it is hard to imagine the impact of these first published royal photographs. For generations people had known the royal family only through engravings, which were often little better than cartoons. Photography added a new dimension to the relationship between monarch and subject. For the first time ordinary people could see exactly what the Queen looked like. They became aware of her family too as real human beings – who wore day clothes, not cloth-of-gold and ermine; who were confident or shy before the camera and whose children often frowned, sulked or fidgeted when told to sit still. The Queen's younger children and her grandchildren and great-grandchildren grew up in front of the camera lens. Their fashions, hairstyles and

Princess Victoria of Wales (posed by a looking-glass). One of sixteen granddaughters of the Queen to have 'Victoria' among their given names. Five of them actually used it.

poses were emulated and it became commonplace to display royal photographs beside the more humble subjects in the family album. The pride and affection was obvious and the message clear; 'they are like us, we can be like them. They are ours.'

The Queen felt the same interest in photographs. She and the Prince collected cartes of the European royal families for their albums. They sought photographic records of significant places and events, and the Queen was also keen to obtain photos of her subjects. In November 1860 Lady Eleanor Stanley, one of the maids-of-honour, told her sister Lady Cremorne, 'I have been writing to all the fine ladies in London, for theirs or their husband's photographs, for the Queen . . . I believe Miss Skerrett is right when she says "she (the Queen) could be bought, and sold for a Photograph!"' Miss Skerrett was the Queen's Dresser and her photograph would have been included in the royal albums too, with courtiers and Household and workers from the various royal estates and their families, for the Queen had no prejudice. She was interested in people, whoever they were, and photography accorded perfectly with her taste for straightforward, real things that could easily be understood. She encouraged her children to take an interest in photography and they also collected. At seventeen years old her youngest son, Leopold, developed a taste for photographs of attractive women from society and the opera. At the end of one 'wants list' to a friend he added, 'You must send me the bill for them or I will ruin myself in photos.'

The mid-1860s saw a new development, the 'cabinet portrait', a card-mounted photograph similar in style to the carte but three times the size. These never sold in quite such numbers, but the larger format made group photographs more practicable and more appealing, and special albums were designed to allow the two sizes to be displayed together. Then the end of the nineteenth century saw the advent of the picture postcard and a whole new dimension to photograph collecting, with everything from large-scale publishers distributing professional studio portraits of the sovereigns of Europe to enterprising local photographers catching a quick snap of a royal visitor. In the Edwardian period postcard collecting was even more widespread than the carte-de-visite collecting of a generation before. The postcard had the added advantage of being a quick and cheap message service. A card posted early in the morning would sometimes arrive the same day, certainly the next. Photography was no longer a novelty, but this was the great age of royalty and the demand was insatiable. Through the First World War and into the period between the wars, royal postcards were sold in their millions. In Germany in the 1930s even the royal and princely families who had been deprived of their thrones – including many of Queen Victoria's descendants – commanded enough sympathy from their former subjects for postcard portraits still to be in demand.

For us today these images continue to have great immediacy and interest. Family history is more popular now than it has even been, and this album is essentially a family history – though the family is larger and more carefully documented than most, and covers a wider range of nationalities and loyalties. The Queen's first child, Vicky, was born in November 1840. She had eight more children: in an age when stillbirths were common and many babies died in infancy Victoria was justly proud of her healthy family. She never understood the haemophilia she had passed to her youngest son, which would wreak such havoc in later generations. She took great pleasure in her children when they were small, delighting in their appearance – sometimes – in their endearing sayings, and in all the little set pieces of family life Prince Albert created for her: the children presenting posies of flowers, performing little plays and recitations, making gestures of affection and tenderness. She found it harder to deal with the signs of independence which inevitably come as children grow: she could never forget that her family lived in the public eye, and that a great deal was expected from them. Her own expectations were correspondingly high.

The Queen and Prince Albert made ambitious plans for their children's marriages, looking out towards the European royal houses and imagining a time when a complicated network of royal relationships would play its own part in securing peace and stability in Europe. These plans changed radically once the Queen was a widow. Then she wanted to keep more of her children near home, both for her own comfort, and because she was wise enough to sense her country's growing antagonism to foreign marriages. Besides, as the years passed it was obvious that the Continent was not developing along the lines her husband had envisaged. War in Europe brought division in the family even in the nineteenth century – the Queen would have been horrified if she had known what was to come in the decades following her death.

While she lived, Victoria held the family together. There were tensions. There were times when one or other of the children was not on good terms with their mother, or when the children argued, but underlying these temporary quarrels was a fundamental strength. Victoria's family were always aware of themselves as a unit. The children kept in touch and supported one another throughout life. However angry they might have been with their mother at times, however critical of her ways, she was still their mother. The bond still held, and the grandchildren were brought up within it. Even the young Prussians – Vicky's elder children –

who grew away from their mother and from all things English were still the Queen's grandchildren, and they knew it. She enjoyed the company of all the family (in small doses) and felt particularly close to her daughters and granddaughters – she was never comfortable with young men and their ways. Victoria died at Osborne on 22 January 1901 surrounded by three generations of her descendants and afterwards, inevitably, some of this family unity was lost. Her children Alice, Alfred and Leopold had died before her; Vicky was dying and would outlive her mother by months only; without the elder generation the family was bound to fragment, remembering but not feeling the same ties.

Royalty is an accident of birth, and the royal family, like all families, had its successes and its tragedies, dilemmas faced and overcome, happy marriages and marriages that failed. Attitudes to the royal family may have changed, in some quarters at least, but their lives still intrigue, and through photographs we can watch them develop and change, becoming more like Uncle so-and-so or an aunt long dead, and taking up an active or an ornamental role in society. Even the sternest critic of royalty could not deny the part Victoria's descendants have played in shaping the world as it is today. Her line includes influential patrons of medicine, science and the arts, social improvers, gifted artists, writers and musicians, military and naval commanders, sportsmen and women and, of course, a fair number of British and European sovereigns – even seven canonised saints. A few of the Queen's descendants became confirmed Nazis in their time, but others have been honoured for their attempts to save Jewish people from the Holocaust. All inherited something from their formidable ancestor, even if it was only the status which they would have to live up to and for which they would always be judged. Many would have wished not to be royal. A few positively enjoyed it. Together their stories add up to a wide-ranging chronicle of an extraordinary ordinary family and the times in which they lived.

1

The Queen and her Children

Queen Victoria and Prince Albert were married in February 1840. Princess Victoria was born the following November and over the next seventeen years the couple would have eight more children; the Prince of Wales, Princess Alice, Prince Alfred, Princesses Helena and Louise, Princes Arthur and Leopold, and finally Princess Beatrice. The Queen was proud of her children — though she did not always find them easy to deal with. She sketched them, painted them, and made enthusiastic use of the new art of photography to record their likenesses and the significant moments in their lives. In 1860, for the first time, she and Prince Albert allowed a selection of specially taken photographs to be made public . . .

The Queen and Prince Albert taken by the American J.J.E. Mayall in May 1860. 'He is the oddest man I know', Victoria wrote, 'but an excellent photographer'. This was one of the first royal photos to be published and the couple chose a consciously domestic image – no crowns, no tiaras, no orders or signs of their rank. They wore mourning for the Queen's brother-in-law, Prince Ernst of Hohenlohe-Langenburg, who died on 12 April, and their pose emphasises seriousness, respectability and mutual dependence – attitudes they liked to adopt before the camera. In 1855 one of Victoria's maids-of-honour told her father, 'We have been amusing ourselves looking at the Queen's private album of photographs . . . the Queen and Prince themselves in every variety of attitude; such as his sitting looking into a book and she with her arm round his neck standing by – or she turning away as if saying no to something, while he is leaning over her as they sit on the sofa as if trying to convince her and bring her round to what he wishes – and many less interesting . . .'

An early Mayall carte of Victoria, Princess Royal, the eldest child, who was always known as 'Vicky'.
When Mayall's *Royal Album* was published she was already a married woman with two children, and
living in Germany.

The Prince of Wales and Princess Alice, who were close to one another from their nursery days. In 1859 Lady Eleanor Stanley noted 'Prince of Wales is improved in looks, I think; grown more manly; he is less like his father in voice and manner, but he will never be so good-looking. . . . He is *very* like Princess Alice: I never saw a stronger likeness between brother and sister; but they are not alike in character at all; he is retiring, shy, a little inclined to be overbearing, and rather obstinate; but with a sweet, kind expression about his eyes; – she, not apparently knowing what shyness means, very sweet-tempered, and not at all obstinate.'

Prince Alfred in his midshipman's uniform. 'Affie' began training for the Navy at the age of twelve, at his own request. He was bright and lively, and very much like his father in looks. 'Prince Alfred is certainly a very nice little fellow, and good looking; but so small!' (this is Lady Eleanor again, writing in 1860) 'and such a pickle! evidently just as full of mischief as an egg is of meat; and I hear the navy are by this time perfectly aware of the fact.'

Princess Helena (standing) and Princess Louise, the third and fourth daughters, who were thrown together because they were close in age, but turned out completely unalike. After the nursery Helena was considered the plain one in the family: 'Lenchen's features are again now so very large and long that it spoils her looks', the Queen complained. She also had problems with her weight. Louise, meanwhile, was reckoned the family beauty – but she was also the most temperamental of the Queen's daughters.

The younger sons, Arthur (right) and Leopold, photographed by Mayall in 1861. Arthur had left the nursery in 1859 and passed into the care of a male governor and Leopold longed to join him, to be seen as a boy and not a baby. His moment came at the start of 1861, much to his delight.

Three-year-old Beatrice in June 1860. Her elaborate little dress, complete with garland, gloves and fan, must have been intended for a special occasion – perhaps the Queen's birthday on 24 May. The children did dress up for family birthdays and anniversaries, and put on recitations, musical performances and plays to entertain their parents – sometimes the Court as well. Beatrice was a great pet. A few weeks after this photo was taken she entertained the Queen's ladies 'with little pieces of poetry, "Twinkle, Twinkle," "Little Miss Muffet," "Humpty Dumpty," and several others, speaking remarkably plainly and nicely, but showing a considerable degree of character in her choice of the poems and her claiming of the rewards (biscuits) for repeating them. She is a most amusing little dot, all the more so for being generally a little naughty . . .'

These early Mayall cartes were popular. People liked owning photographs of the royal family and wanted to see more: by the last quarter of the century they were able to extend their collections backwards with copy prints of earlier royal portraits. Here Victoria appears as a young mother in the spring of 1842, with Vicky and the baby Prince of Wales. The original painting by Landseer was given to the Queen by Prince Albert on her twenty-third birthday.

This photo of the Prince of Wales, based on a portrait by Winterhalter, marks a turning point in children's fashion. It was 1846 and the four-year-old was given a scaled-down version of the uniform worn by ratings on the Royal Yacht. He wore it during a cruise off the Channel Islands in September, delighting his mother and the public alike. Popular engravings spread the idea and by the 1870s the sailor suit had become normal dress for boys all over the world – and often for their sisters too. The original suit is preserved in the National Maritime Museum at Greenwich.

From the royal family's private albums: this daguerreotype of the Queen with her five eldest children was taken in about 1852 – perhaps a year or so earlier. Vicky is on the right with the handbag, next to the Prince of Wales: Alice has her hand on Affie's shoulder and Helena rests her head on her mother's knee – a favourite pose which would be repeated by successive generations of royal children. The Queen has turned her head away from the camera: she was rather conscious of her appearance in these early photos, and at a later sitting complained that her portrait had not turned out well.

Princess Helena (left) and Princess Louise in costume for 'Les Petits Savoyards', which was staged by the royal children and several other children from the Court at Windsor in February 1854. 'I never saw anything so pretty as the little children's play on Friday evening, so nicely acted,' Lady Eleanor Stanley told her father, 'and the little stage and all the dresses so beautifully got up, of course regardless of expense. . . . really the whole thing was most beautiful.'

More costumes, this time for the costume ball held at Buckingham Palace on 7 April 1859 for Prince Leopold's sixth birthday, when he and Prince Arthur (Leopold is standing in this photo, and Arthur sitting down) were dressed as the sons of King Henry IV. It was a glamorous occasion, reported in the society papers: two hundred guests aged between six and fourteen danced through the evening, watched by their parents, until supper was held – at midnight.

The entertainments ended with the death of Prince Albert, at Windsor on 14 December 1861. It would be some time before Victoria could involve herself wholeheartedly in acting or dancing again. The Prince was a strict father, sometimes rather too high-minded, but parenthood came more naturally to him than it did to the Queen and he devoted a great deal of time, energy and affection to his children. The nine were Victoria's children but they were also Albert's, with a good deal of their father in them.

The Queen, Vicky (behind), Alice (kneeling) and Alfred, mourning the Prince; a photo taken at Windsor in March 1862, shortly after the Queen's return from Osborne, where she had taken refuge in the first weeks of her widowhood. The group is dominated by the larger-than-life bust of Prince Albert gazing out of the picture towards the light. Under one print of this photograph Victoria wrote the words, 'Day turned into night'.

Occasions when all nine children came together were rare. This photo was taken in August 1865 at the Rosenau in Coburg, where the family had gathered for the unveiling of a statue of Prince Albert. By this time Vicky, Alice and Bertie, the Prince of Wales, were all married. They are in the centre of the group which shows (l to r) Leopold (who had fallen on the Royal Yacht on the way to Germany and injured his knee. He was unable to stand – hence the chair), Louise, Beatrice, Alice, Bertie, Arthur (on the ground), Vicky, Affie and Helena.

The Queen at Balmoral in 1867 with her dog, Sharp.

Vicky in the 1860s. A precocious child, quick-witted and always conscious of her standing as the eldest in the family, the Princess Royal was very much her father's child. He undertook the later stages of her education himself and fired an interest in politics and social reform which stayed with her for the rest of her life. She could be opinionated and judgemental at times but was supportive to her family, and her massive correspondence with the Queen – they wrote to each other almost every day – is our most important source on the private lives of the royal family. Vicky was a gifted artist whose painting and sculpture was exhibited alongside the work of professionals.

Bertie, the Prince of Wales, at Abergeldie in September 1886. His life would have been easier, in childhood and beyond, if he had been more like his father. But the rigorous, intellectual regime Prince Albert had designed for him was totally unsuitable: the Prince of Wales was a 'people' person who thrived on friendship and society. His father failed to understand the potential in this, so too did his mother, who feared the likenesses she sensed between her eldest son and her Hanover uncles. She refused to allow her son access to affairs of State, forcing him to develop a role for himself – which in time he did, with considerable success.

If Vicky possessed her father's intellect, Alice inherited his conscience. From the first weeks of her married life she devoted herself to the welfare of her adopted country, visiting the poorest homes incognito to see conditions and offer practical help. Nursing was her first good cause, also the education, employment and health of women. She was a gifted pianist too and fascinated by philosophy – her son would later remember her for her sense of humour but the camera only ever captured the underlying seriousness of her nature.

Prince Alfred in the late 1860s. Affie was the first member of the Queen's family to experience the unfortunate consequences of the fact that Prince Albert's brother Ernst, Duke of Saxe-Coburg-Gotha, had no children. Affie became the heir, which did not sit easily with his life as a career sailor in the British Navy, a life he really enjoyed. In 1864 he tried to renounce his rights to Coburg, wavered, and then changed his mind. It might have been better for him and for later generations of the royal family if he had stuck to his original decision.

Despite her mother's criticism, Princess Helena was rather attractive as a young woman. She was clever too, being particularly gifted in languages: in 1887 she published a translation of the writings of the Margravine of Bayreuth, and she also published a memoir of her sister Alice. She loved music and gave her time and energies to a number of charities, but her dominant interest, and the one for which she is generally remembered, was nursing. She worked hard to advance the state of nursing in this country and institutions with the name 'Princess Christian's . . .' (her married name) are her lasting legacy.

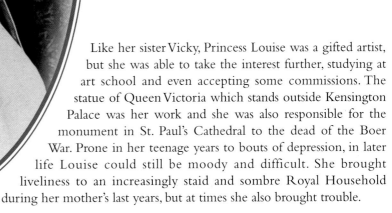

Like her sister Vicky, Princess Louise was a gifted artist, but she was able to take the interest further, studying at art school and even accepting some commissions. The statue of Queen Victoria which stands outside Kensington Palace was her work and she was also responsible for the monument in St. Paul's Cathedral to the dead of the Boer War. Prone in her teenage years to bouts of depression, in later life Louise could still be moody and difficult. She brought liveliness to an increasingly staid and sombre Royal Household during her mother's last years, but at times she also brought trouble.

Prince Arthur was the Queen's acknowledged favourite – 'this child is dear, *dearer*, than any of the others put together,' she told Prince Albert in 1858 – and unlike his older brothers he never did anything to disappoint her. Destined for the army from birth – as a toddler he was encouraged to remind people that the Duke of Wellington was his godfather – he entered the Royal Military Academy at Woolwich in 1867 and received his first commission a year later. The second photo (below) was taken in Canada where the Prince stayed from August 1869 until July 1870, twice visiting the USA. Briefly, he saw active service during the visit when a group of Fenians – Irish nationalists – attempted an invasion from American territory. In 1911 he was to become Governor-General of Canada, a post he held for five years.

Leopold was the first member of the Queen's family to suffer from haemophilia. If his father had lived, Leopold would have been educated with Arthur, but the Queen's worries about his health combined with her determination to keep two children perpetually by her side – Leopold as her assistant and Beatrice her companion – put an end to this plan. He was a lonely boy, perpetually reaching out to the world which fate and his mother denied him. He was also the most academic of the Queen's sons and in 1872, on his own insistence and much against the Queen's wishes, he became a student at Oxford. This introduced him to some of the finest minds in the country and broadened his horizons: after Oxford he became increasingly active in public life, supporting a wide range of social, medical and artistic causes. The tense relationship with his mother lasted for the rest of his life.

The 'amusing little dot' of the 1860s, with her nursery rhymes and cheeky charm, Princess Beatrice was drawn entirely into her mother's world. Photographs like these, taken in her teens, show that she was still very attractive, but she became increasingly plump and painfully shy. Like Helena, whom she most closely resembled, Beatrice was a gifted pianist and linguist. In 1941 she published a translation of the diary of her great-grandmother, Duchess Augusta of Saxe-Coburg-Saalfield, but she will always be remembered for her editing of the Queen's journals and destruction of the original volumes, a task which took her thirty years.

2

Engagements and Weddings

The Queen and Prince Albert placed great importance on the marriages of their children. They would arrange these themselves, but for the child's happiness and with the child's agreement. The Prince's plans were focused on the elder children and the parts he wanted them to play in the political development of Europe. He died too soon to assist that development – or to make decisions for his younger children.

Balmoral, 29 September 1855; the Queen and Prince Albert (centre right) with Vicky (beside her father), the Prince of Wales and Alice (next to their mother), Prince Friedrich Wilhelm of Prussia and Affie. It was on this day that Prince Friedrich Wilhelm proposed to Vicky and was, rather shyly, accepted. He had spoken beforehand to her parents and been asked to say nothing until the following year, after the Princess's confirmation, but he had already waited a long time and his courtship took on a momentum that no one could stop – even if they had wanted to. The engagement remained private until the following year.

Opposite: Vicky and Friedrich Wilhelm, 'Fritz', together in the early 1860s. It was an arranged marriage. The very idea of a fourteen-year-old being manoeuvred so deliberately towards a man of twenty-three is uncomfortable by modern standards, but the surprising truth is that Vicky fell in love by arrangement and remained devoted to her husband for more than thirty years. Their problems were political. The marriage was viewed with suspicion in England and hated in Prussia, where the little Princess with her English ways and progressive ideas never found acceptance. Her father would have been horrified if he could have seen how far from the real world his idea of Germany became.

Princess Alice, taken by Mayall on 1 June 1861.

Willem, Prince of Orange, 'the Orange boy', was Albert's first choice as a husband for Alice. Willem was two months older than the Princess Royal and heir to the throne of the Netherlands – the eldest son of King Willem III and Queen Sophie. His family background was miserably unhappy. His father was cold to his mother, openly unfaithful and often violent. She was hypersensitive and emotional. In the early 1850s they agreed to a legal separation: after this Willem was seldom allowed to see his mother at all. His father showed little interest and the rumours that Willem led a dissolute life were probably true, even as early 1860. Victoria and Albert were prepared to make allowances, at first, but the meeting with Alice was not a success. Later he opted out of royal duties altogether and set up home in Paris. After Alice's marriage to Ludwig of Hesse-Darmstadt he was mentioned as a possible husband for Helena or Louise but Queen Victoria would never have considered him – in the event, he remained unmarried.

Prince Ludwig of Hesse-Darmstadt, 'Louis', proved a much more likely candidate. He visited England in the summer of 1860 with his younger brother, made a good impression, and returned in November. 'Princess Alice and her Louis seem getting on very swimmingly;' Lady Eleanor Stanley told her sister on 28 November, 'she looked awfully shy and blushing the first day or two, but seems much less so now and very happy. . . . He is not handsome . . . still, he looks honest and good, and I think on the whole, the Queen and Prince were right in deciding for her.'

Like her elder sister, Alice had to wait some time before she could marry: while she waited her father died, and the wedding, at Osborne on 1 July 1862, was a strained and sad affair. It was the Queen's intention that Alice and her husband should spend much of their time in England and they did, at first, though Louis had duties in his own country, where his childless uncle reigned as Grand Duke, and Alice's relationship with her mother became increasingly difficult. Louis was devoted to Alice. She loved him too, though there were times in later years when she longed to communicate on a deeper level than her bluff, good-natured husband seemed able to achieve.

The challenge for Victoria and Albert was to find a bride for their eldest son before he strayed into the bad ways which had characterised his Hanoverian great-uncles. The Queen enlisted the help of the Princess Royal, now settled in Germany and in a good position to observe suitable princesses: 'God knows! where the young lady we want is to be found! Good looks, health, education, character, intellect and a good disposition we want; great rank and riches we do not.'

Princess Elisabeth of Wied was one of the first candidates for Bertie. She was a dreamy, romantic girl who led a very sheltered life, writing poetry and caring for her handicapped younger brother, who died in 1862. The Queen heard well of her at first and, although Vicky was not impressed, Elisabeth remained in contention for some time. But she had a worrying tendency to discuss unsuitable subjects and her dress sense was poor. Later Elisabeth would be considered for Prince Alfred, but her fate lay elsewhere. In 1869 she married Prince Karl of Hohenzollern-Sigmaringen, becoming his consort when he was elected Prince, and then King, of a newly independent Romania. Elisabeth also made a name for herself as a writer, publishing as 'Carmen Sylva'.

Meanwhile, for the Prince of Wales, the Queen's attention turned to Denmark. She and Prince Albert were very reluctant to take this course; they had reservations about Prince Christian and Princess Louise, the prospective bride's parents, even though Christian was in line for the Danish throne. But Alexandra, the couple's elder daughter, had a beauty and personality which recommended her from the start, and once Bertie had met her the decision was inescapable. The photograph shows Alexandra on the left, with her parents and her younger sister Dagmar, later to become Tsaritsa of Russia.

Alexandra on her wedding day, 10 March 1863.

The bust of Prince Albert presiding over his changing family: a photograph taken soon after the wedding of the Prince and Princess of Wales which shows, from the left, Louise, Alexandra, the Prince of Wales, the Queen with Beatrice and Leopold, Alice, Helena and Louis of Hesse-Darmstadt. Groups like this emphasised Prince Albert's continued presence but in fact, the marriage of the Prince of Wales was the last alliance they had discussed and agreed together. Decisions concerning the younger children would depend on the Queen alone.

Helena was next to marry. For several years she had acted as companion and assistant to her mother, and the Queen was determined to keep her in England. The Princess Royal suggested Prince Elimar of Oldenburg for her but nothing came of a visit he made to Balmoral. On 5 July 1866 Helena was married in the private chapel at Windsor to Prince Christian of Schleswig-Holstein-Augustenburg – a man fifteen years older than herself with no prospects of his own, who was happy to settle in this country. There was some opposition from within the family but the marriage was happy and lasting.

John Campbell, Marquess of Lorne, heir to the 8th Duke of Argyll. The Queen's acceptance of a British nobleman – Lorne – as a husband for Louise caused even greater outrage, particularly in Prussia where marriage between a princess and a commoner was unthinkable. Most of the continental royal families had strict rules governing who was and was not suitable for their children – a prince could contract a legal marriage with someone outside his own class, but his wife and children would be shunned at royal events and the children would have no dynastic rights. Queen Victoria had no time for 'morganatic' marriages. For her a marriage was either legal, or it was not. With five children still unmarried she sensed the British public's resistance to the constant stream of foreign princes and princesses, all requiring an income. It was her idea to consider the British aristocracy – those with money, at least – and she was not to be put off, even by her own family.

Princess Louise and Lord Lorne were married in St George's Chapel, Windsor, on 21 March 1871.

Princess Frederica, 'Lily', of Hanover attracted Affie, who embarked on his search for a bride in the spring of 1864. But the Queen put him off. She believed that her Hanover cousins were afflicted by hereditary blindness and other complaints, and her doctor backed her up. Frederica's name would come up again in the spring of 1878 when Leopold went abroad, against his mother's wishes, and visited the Hanover family. Frederica was five years older than Leopold: nonetheless, he was allowed to return later in the year to assess his chances. Finding that Frederica was in love with her father's secretary, whom her family would not allow her to marry, he returned home to enlist the Queen's help. She could give permission for the marriage and she did, providing a home for the couple at Hampton Court. Frederica remained a good friend to the Queen's younger children.

It was Princess Alice who found a bride for Prince Alfred. Grand Princess Maria Alexandrovna of Russia (seen here in Russian Court dress) was a cousin of Louis of Hesse-Darmstadt and a regular visitor to Darmstadt. Alice liked her and introduced her to Affie, doing her best to encourage the courtship. The Queen was persuaded to accept – much against her will. She disliked the idea of a Russian marriage, partly because of the Crimean War and partly because her aunt, Princess Juliane of Saxe-Coburg, had been very unhappily married to Maria's great-uncle, Grand Prince Konstantin. But the Queen missed Affie's wedding, which was celebrated in the Winter Palace in St Petersburg on 23 January 1874.

Maria's father, Tsar Alexander II of Russia (seated), with his fourth son Alexei Alexandrovich (left), Maria and Affie, taken on a visit to England in May 1874.

The Princess of Wales (right) with her youngest sister Thyra. Prince Arthur remembered Thyra from the Wales' wedding, and in 1872 he expressed a wish to meet her again. But she had come close to death from typhoid in Italy that spring and her mother thought it best to postpone the meeting – Thyra was still painfully thin and had lost all her hair. Arthur did not see her until the summer of 1873, and must have been disappointed. Nothing more was said, and in 1878 Thyra married the Crown Prince of Hanover, Frederica's brother.

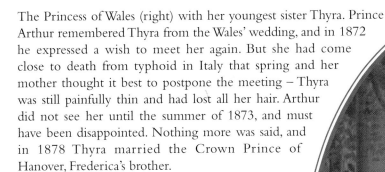

Marie of Hanover, Frederica's younger sister, caught Arthur's eye in 1875. She did not return his feelings and the negotiations came to nothing. Marie never married.

Arthur (left) in 1878 with his fiancée Luise Margarete of Prussia and her sisters, Marie (centre, with her husband Prince Hendrik of the Netherlands) and Elisabeth (right, with her husband Duke Friedrich August of Oldenburg). The Queen was combing the Peerage for a partner for Arthur when Vicky introduced him to Luise Margarete, on a visit to Berlin in 1878. He was delighted, and although the Queen had reservations about Luise Margarete's parents she did not refuse him.

Princess Luise Margarete, Duchess of Connaught, on her wedding day, 13 March 1879.

The happiest engagement photo of them all: Prince Leopold with Princess Helen of Waldeck in November 1881. After Arthur's marriage only two children remained and the Queen was determined that they would never marry. She wanted to keep Leopold and Beatrice, preserving a last, faint echo of the family circle Prince Albert had created for her. She had convinced herself that they too would be happy, but they were no longer children. Leopold saw marriage as his only hope of independence and he needed the personal assurance only marriage could give. None of the Queen's children would search more desperately than he did. Any prospective bride must be told about his haemophilia: for most, this was enough. His unhappiness persuaded his mother to help him, against her better judgement, and in 1881 she suggested a meeting with Helen. It could not have been more successful.

In the spring of 1884, the Queen set out for Darmstadt for the wedding of Alice's eldest daughter, Victoria of Hesse-Darmstadt. Alice had been dead six years and her mother took a protective interest in the Hesse children; she had even been persuaded to consider a marriage between Beatrice and their widowed father, but this proved to be unlawful. By 1884 she felt completely secure in her possession of Beatrice, so she was horrified to learn that her youngest daughter had fallen in love during the wedding celebrations with the bridegroom's brother, Prince Henry of Battenberg. For six months she refused to speak to Beatrice at all, but finally she relented, on condition that Henry would resign his army commission and settle in England.

The Queen was annoyed only because she wanted to keep Beatrice to herself. Her consent is clear evidence of her broad-mindedness in the matter of marriage, for the Battenbergs were a morganatic family and most royal houses would have disdained them. This group was taken at Osborne around the time of the wedding in July 1885 and shows the Battenberg family as the Queen's honoured guests: (behind) Marie of Battenberg, Princess Gustav of Erbach-Schönberg; Prince Alexander of Battenberg; Prince Alexander of Hesse-Darmstadt (their father); Prince Henry of Battenberg; Prince Gustav of Erbach-Schönberg; Princess Beatrice; Prince Franz Josef of Battenberg (partly hidden); Grand Duke Louis of Hesse-Darmstadt; Prince Louis of Battenberg. In front are: Princesses Irene and Alix of Hesse-Darmstadt, Alice's younger daughters who were to be Beatrice's bridesmaids; Julie, Princess of Battenberg; Ernst Ludwig of Hesse-Darmstadt and his sister Victoria, Princess Louis of Battenberg with her daughter Alice. Prince Alexander of Hesse was an uncle of Affie's wife, who had lost his standing at the Russian Court by insisting on marriage to a maid-of-honour (the lady in the centre of the picture). The marriage had to be morganatic so the children had nothing but their looks to recommend them. The Prussians were horrified that Queen Victoria was prepared to see Beatrice married to a Battenberg, but the Queen ignored them and welcomed Prince Henry and his family without prejudice – though they had had a terrible journey across the Channel and had all been so sea-sick that they hardly knew where they were.

3

Family life

Victoria and Albert became grandparents at the age of thirty-nine with the birth of Vicky's first child. There would be thirty-nine more grandchildren in time, though only Victoria would live to see them all. She would also have twenty-nine great-grandchildren before the end of her long life.

Vicky with her first two children, Wilhelm (standing) and Charlotte. The carte-de-viste, by Mayall, is dated 1 December 1861 but the actual photo must be a few months earlier: Vicky and her family had visited England in July and she wears mourning for the Duchess of Kent, the Queen's mother, who died on 16 March. Wilhelm's birth, in January 1859, had been a desperate affair. Vicky had been in labour for over eight hours when it was discovered that the baby was in the breech position. It was too late to turn him: the ordeal lasted more than four hours longer until, with the baby apparently wedged, half in half out, and deprived of oxygen, and Vicky at the end of her strength, one of the doctors forced the birth. He saved both their lives, but in pulling the baby free he caused irreparable damage to the nerves of Wilhelm's shoulder and neck. One arm was paralysed at first and never grew properly and Wilhelm, who was otherwise a pretty child, developed a series of minor facial deformities. He carried his head on one side and was required to undergo a long programme of treatments – everything from operations and the wearing of a 'stretching-machine' to thrusting the paralysed arm into the body of a newly-killed hare. He would later blame his mother for all he endured, but she was in a position where she could not do right: at the Prussian Court her every move was watched and criticised, and she was still little more than a child herself.

Wilhelm with his aunt, Princess Beatrice at Osborne in 1862.

Vicky and Fritz in 1865 with Wilhelm (behind his mother: the damaged arm is hidden, as it would often be in photographs), Charlotte (in white), Heinrich, 'Henry', and Sigismund (in his father's arms). Vicky had difficulties with each of the three elder children. Charlotte she thought backward and rather like her own sister Louise, who was, she said, 'very odd; dreadfully contradictory, very indiscreet and, from that, making mischief very frequently.' Henry at this age, 'cries and grumbles more than any child I ever came near.' He had a favourite saying, 'You look like a Regent Street swell', picked up from his English nurses.

Alice went home to give birth to her first child, Victoria, who was born at Windsor on 5 April 1863 with the Queen on hand to give comfort and reassurance. 'I thought it the most dreadful thing to witness – possible', the Queen wrote. 'Quite awful! I had far rather have gone through it myself.' This photo of Alice and baby Victoria was taken in Scotland.

Alexandra, Princess of Wales, with her first child Prince Albert Victor on a visit to her family in Denmark. Albert Victor was the Queen's most important grandchild, second in line to the British throne. But his birth was premature and nothing had been prepared: his mother went into labour after watching her husband play ice hockey on the frozen lake at Frogmore. One of her ladies helped the local doctor to deliver the baby who weighed less than four pounds. He was wrapped in cotton wadding and flannel hastily bought from the local draper.

Alice and Louis with their first two daughters, Victoria (beside Louis) and Elisabeth, 'Ella', in England in about 1867. Alice enjoyed her children and spent a lot of time with them, fascinated by all aspects of their development. Her letters home were full of observations of their characters and the differences between them. In December 1867 she told her mother, 'Ella, who was breakfasting with me just now, saw me dip my *Bretzel* in my coffee, and said: 'Oh, Mama, you must not! Do you allow yourself to do that?' because I don't allow her to do it. She is too funny, and by no means quite easy to manage – a great contrast to Victoria, who is a very tractable child.'

The Prince and Princess of Wales at Abergeldie in 1868 with Albert Victor, 'Eddy', (centre), George and Louise. These early photographic sessions involved a number of poses and must have taken some time. In this case little Prince George has obviously had enough!

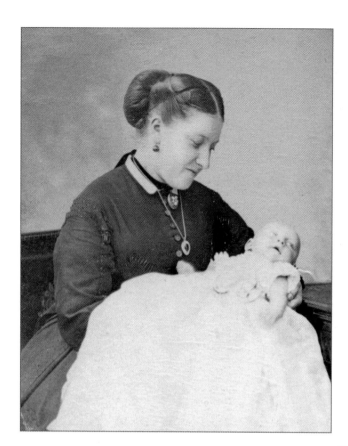

Helena with her first baby, Prince Christian Victor of Schleswig-Holstein, born at Windsor on 14 April 1867.

Prince Christian Victor with his father Prince Christian, c. 1869. 'What a nice, dear little thing he seems', Vicky had written to the Queen, 'but who is he like? Neither Lenchen nor Christian I should think by the photograph.' In time he came to resemble both parents, particularly his father, and he is said to have inherited the absolute truthfulness which was the Queen's most striking feature.

The Queen with Albert Victor (left) and George of Wales, Victoria (standing) and Ella of Hesse-Darmstadt in the winter of 1871. In the early years of her widowhood the Queen seemed almost overwhelmed by her children's growing families. When the Princess of Wales produced a fourth child in the summer of 1868 she said, 'I fear the seventh grand-daughter and fourteenth grand-child becomes a very uninteresting thing – for me it seems to go on like the rabbits in Windsor Park!' But however distant she felt from the grandchildren as a group, individually she took close interest in them. Victoria of Hesse-Darmstadt remembered this visit: all the children caught whooping-cough and spent weeks in the old nurseries of Buckingham Palace, coughing and examining the toys of the previous generation. Once they were better they joined the Queen at Windsor where they were able to run wild in the corridors with their aunt Beatrice, who was still only thirteen, playing noisy games and stealing biscuits from a table outside the Queen's room.

Prince Christian Victor (right) and Prince Albert of Schleswig-Holstein, *c.* 1876. Helena's children grew up at Cumberland Lodge in Windsor Great Park and enjoyed a happy, uncomplicated childhood. The boys' first tutor, the poet F.W. Bourdillon, remembered, 'My first impression of them was, I think, of brightness, quickness and insatiable curiosity. Prince Christian Victor in particular was never tired of asking questions, and 'why' was almost incessantly on his lips. . . . He was, moreover, a most attaching, lovable boy, whom it was impossible not to get fond of immediately.' Lady Bancroft, who played host to both boys during a holiday in 1880 and nursed Christian Victor when he became ill, described Prince Albert as 'a very clever, sharp boy, full of spirits and of mischief. He was a wonderful mimic. One day when I was busily engaged in measuring and mixing a dose for my patient, I could see reflected in the looking glass Prince 'Abby' at the other end of the room imitating my every movement. I was so amused that I purposely took longer over mixing, measuring and shaking than I need have done, and invented movements in order to draw him on. . . . At last I could hold out no longer, and I laughed heartily.'

Their younger sisters, Helena Victoria (right) and Marie Louise of Schleswig-Holstein. Marie Louise was actually christened 'Francisca Josepha Louise Augusta Marie Hélène Christina': at first the family called her 'Louise', later she chose her own version of her name.

Alice's children: (l to r) Irene, Ernst Ludwig, Marie ('May'), Victoria, Alix (in front) and Ella in about 1875. A younger son, Friedrich Wilhelm, born between Alix and May, had died as the result of an accident at the Neues Palais in Darmstadt in 1873. Returning home after a summer of holidays and visits in 1874 Alice told her mother, 'Ella is another child since she has been at the seaside – fine colour, no longer pale and languid, learns well, and is quite different. Ernie the same, bright and fresh; while before they had been looking pulled and weak, outgrowing their strength.

"Sunny' [Alix] is the picture of robust health, and sweet little 'sister Maly' sits up quite alone, and is very neat and rosy, with such quick eyes, and two deep dimples in her cheeks – a great pet, and so like my poor Frittie.

'The return here has been very painful, and days of great depression still come, when I am tormented with the dreadful remembrance of the day I lost him. Too cruel and agonising are those thoughts. I dwell on his rest and peace, and that our sufferings he cannot know. What might not life have brought him? Better so! but hard to say, 'God's will be done"

Vicky and Fritz with Charlotte (left), Victoria (in front), Waldemar, Sophie (beside her mother) and Margarete (in her father's arms), in about 1875. Wilhelm and Henry are missing from the photograph; so is Sigismund, who had died in 1866. Vicky was more at ease with motherhood by the time her younger children were born. She was more grown-up herself, of course, and had come to terms with the difficulties of her life in Prussia and she enjoyed the younger children. They, in turn, grew closer to her while the three eldest drew further and further away.

Prince Alfred and Grand Princess Maria, Duke and Duchess of Edinburgh, with their first child Prince Alfred, 'young Alfred', born at Buckingham Palace in October 1874. 'It is very good and is a fine child,' the Queen told her eldest daughter, 'large and fat and fair while Affie was dark; I . . . think it will become very large and like its enormous Russian uncles. It seems very good tempered, but is greedy . . .'

The Edinburgh children in 1880: (l to r) Victoria Melita, Alexandra (in front), Alfred and Marie. The Duchess of Edinburgh was raised in a tradition of royal life and behaviour a world away from that of the Queen. In St Petersburg the imperial family was expected to lead society. Their extravagant palaces and conspicuous displays of wealth contributed to a sense of national pride and importance. Whether individual members of the family liked this life-style or not – and some certainly did not – they had to play their part. The Duchess was a strict mother. She expected great self discipline, even from the youngest child. So her children were well behaved, which made them popular within the family, particularly with the Queen; 'We have dear Uncle Alfred's darling little children here wh is a gt pleasure,' she told one of her other granddaughters in 1880, 'they are such lovely children.' But they also learned or imbibed a sense of their own importance, above that of other people – and this was something Victoria would not have encouraged.

The Princess of Wales with her children in 1879: (l to r) Victoria, Albert Victor, the Princess, Maud (sitting), Louise, George.

Hereditary Grand Duke Ernst Ludwig of Hesse-Darmstadt with his aunt Princess Louise in 1881. Louise was the only one of the Queen's children to have no family of her own. She minded, particularly envying her sisters Helena and Beatrice their sons – perhaps also their happy marriages. At times she could be spiteful to them, but she enjoyed a better relationship with her brothers and with her nephews and nieces. She was Ernst Ludwig's favourite aunt. In the 1930s he remembered, 'She was so nice to us children, and it always gave her pleasure if she could do things with us. She was beautiful and I worshipped her . . . we could talk over so many things together. She has always remained the same to me, and now when she is almost ninety, she is still a match for any beautiful woman.'

A family gathering in Darmstadt in September 1882. Even without knowing the people concerned it would be possible to separate the family groups here simply by the costumes. It was fashionable for sisters to dress alike, even as grown women. The photo shows (l to r) Prince Albert Victor of Wales; Princess Helena; Princess Alix of Hesse-Darmstadt with the Princess of Wales – Princess Maud of Wales is seated on the floor in front, next to Prince Albert of Schleswig-Holstein; Prince Ernst Ludwig of Hesse-Darmstadt is behind, resting his chin on his hand; the Prince of Wales; Princesses Victoria, Ella and Irene of Hesse-Darmstadt (on the floor); Princess Louise of Wales; Prince Christian; Prince George of Wales; Prince Christian Victor of Schleswig-Holstein; Princess Victoria of Wales; Grand Duke Louis of Hesse-Darmstadt.

Prince Arthur and Princess Luise Margarete, Duke and Duchess of Connaught, with their children Margaret (standing) and Arthur, in Scotland in October 1883.

The Queen with Princess Margaret, 'Daisy', of Connaught in 1884–5. By this time Victoria had become accustomed to the size of her family and she took real pleasure in the younger grandchildren. She wrote that Daisy was 'a great darling – & such a pretty little thing'.

Prince Leopold and Princess Helen, Duke and Duchess of Albany, with their daughter Alice, born at Windsor on 25 February 1883. Leopold was overjoyed to be a father and little Alice became the centre of her parents' life, sitting in her high chair during adult mealtimes and playing in the Drawing-room when visitors were present; it was all very far removed from the secluded nursery her father had known. In November one of Leopold's friends told his mother, 'The baby is most advanced & sits up in a chair to eat toast & Jam! It is a very fine child & scarcely ever cries & is most attached to its parents. It is the very image of the Queen & to me this likeness was startling – in fact I felt quite afraid of the imp.'

In March 1886 the Connaughts had a new baby, Patricia, seen here in her mother's arms while Arthur peers over his father's shoulder and Daisy sits on his knee.

The Duke and Duchess of Connaught with Arthur, Daisy (standing) and Patricia, 'Patsy' in 1893.

Prince Leopold went to Cannes on doctor's orders in February 1884: joint pain is a common symptom of haemophilia and the winter climate in England was always difficult for him. He was also in trouble with his mother, having tried to enlist ministerial support for his appointment to a colonial governorship – even as a married man, he still felt the need to prove himself in the wider world. At the last moment Helen was forced to stay behind. She was pregnant and had already lost a child the previous summer, but she urged him to go. On 27 March he slipped and fell in the Yacht Club in Cannes, injuring his knee and he died in the early hours of the next morning, apparently from the combined effects of the morphine he had been given and the claret that was served with his supper. It came as a terrible shock to all the family, but particularly to Helen. On 19 July 1884 she gave birth to her child, a son, who was given the names Leopold Charles Edward George Albert: after the first few months he was always known as 'Charlie'. The title 2nd Duke of Albany was his from birth.

Alice and Charlie on board the Royal Yacht.

Princess Beatrice and Prince Henry of Battenberg with their first child Alexander, born at Windsor on 23 November 1886.

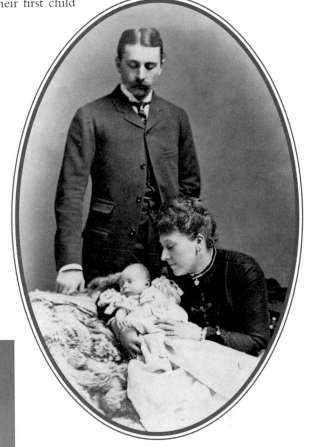

The Queen with the Battenbergs in 1889; Henry holds his son Alexander, 'Drino', while Beatrice has their only daughter Ena (Victoria Eugenie Julia Ena) on her knee. For the Queen the little Battenbergs were very much the 'children of the house', always with her and allowed to play in her room while she worked. In the summer of 1889 Princess Victoria of Prussia was staying in England and wrote home to her mother, 'Drino and Ena are delightful together. She runs about all over the place & the Indians & nurses after her to try & get her back, she is so strong.'

Mealtime at Windsor in 1895: the Queen sits at table with Beatrice and Henry and three of their four children – Leopold (left, on the booster cushion), Alexander (facing his grandmother) and Ena. The rather solemn little party is attended by two of the Indian servants.

Vicky at Friedrichshof in 1898 with her younger daughters and their families: (l to r along the wall) Prince Friedrich Karl of Hesse-Cassel (Margarete's husband); Margarete; Constantine, Duke of Sparta (heir to the throne of Greece and Sophie's husband); Prince Max of Baden (a close friend of Prince Friedrich Karl, who brought Margarete and Friedrich Karl together); Sophie; Victoria and her husband Adolf of Schaumburg-Lippe. In front: Princes Maximilian and Friedrich Wilhelm of Hesse-Cassel; Princes George and Alexander of Greece; Vicky; Princess Helen of Greece.

Opposite: By the 1890s the Queen's first grandchildren were adults with children of their own. This group of the Wales family was taken in 1895–6 and shows, from the left, Alexander, Duke of Fife (husband of Princess Louise of Wales); Louise; George, holding his baby son Edward; the Prince of Wales; the Princess of Wales (sitting); Princess Victoria Mary, 'May', Duchess of York (George's wife); Maud; Victoria (sitting); Prince Carl of Denmark (Maud's fiancé).

The Queen at Balmoral in 1899 with, from the left, Princess Ena of Battenberg, Princess Victoria Melita of Edinburgh, Grand Duchess of Hesse-Darmstadt, her daughter Elisabeth, the Queen, Princess Helena Victoria of Schleswig-Holstein, Prince Maurice of Battenberg. The Queen is said to have felt especially protective towards little Elisabeth of Hesse-Darmstadt because she knew that her parents' marriage was tense and unhappy. Elisabeth's parents were both grandchildren of the Queen.

King Edward VII and Queen Alexandra with their daughter Victoria and grandchildren Mary, Albert (sitting), baby Henry and Edward of Wales, not long after the Queen's death in 1901.

4

The Nursery

The Queen's youngest child was less than two years older than her first grandchild. By the time her youngest grandchild was born she was already a great-grandmother several times over. Within ten years of her death there was a new generation, the great-great-grandchildren of the Queen. Victoria's descendants flourished in nurseries across Europe, from St Petersburg to Bucharest to Madrid to Stockholm and from one end of Germany to the other – and, of course, in England – but wherever they lived their upbringing was surprisingly similar. Old photographs of royal children have a timeless appeal, capturing clothes, toys, all the paraphernalia of childhood, and moments and emotions familiar to us all.

The Queen with her grandson Alexander of Battenberg in 1887. In her later years Victoria was more relaxed with babies and took a close interest in their growth and care. In a taped interview in the 1960s Miss Dorothy Blake, who was born within days of Alexander on the Osborne Estate, where her father was the agent, described how the Queen on her daily visits to the agent's house, Barton Manor, would ask to see the baby; 'and she would take me in her arms and feel my weight, and she would say "Prince Alexander is not as heavy as this; now, Mrs Blake, what is the food?", and my mother would say, "Mellin's Food, your Majesty", and the Queen would say, "I shall have to speak to Prince Alexander's nurses about this." She was always interested in homely detail.'

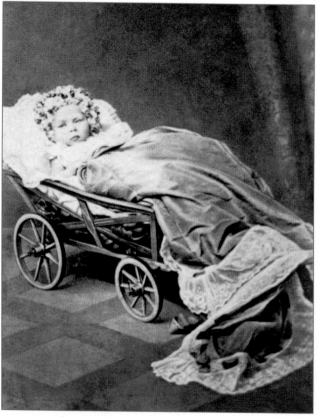

Vicky's eldest daughter Charlotte of Prussia in 1861, in a rather primitive-looking baby carriage. The first perambulator was made in America in 1848 and the idea caught on after the Great Exhibition, but that was a three-wheeler – called a 'Victoria' – with the child sitting up and facing forwards and the adult pushing from behind.

In 1867 the Wales children had a push-chair to gladden the heart of any child, complete with horse and harness. The baby here is Princess Louise of Wales, the Prince's eldest daughter.

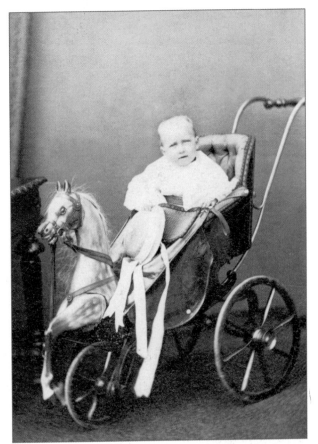

A generation later Louise's daughters, the Ladies Alexandra and Maud Duff, are perched rather awkwardly on something that looks like a decorative wheelbarrow made out of cane. It has proper springs and a handle, but the child in front would be in a precarious position if it was tipped up to move forward. After their grandfather's accession, Alexandra and Maud were raised to the rank of princess. Their mother became the Princess Royal.

Grand Princess Olga Nikolaevna of Russia, Alice's granddaughter, with her nursery maid Maria in 1897. Maria Vishniakova entered the imperial household shortly before the birth of Olga's younger sister Tatiana, and nursed each of the children in turn. They loved her, but in 1910 her claim to have been assaulted by Rasputin soured her relationship with the children's mother, Alice's daughter Alix. Maria's duties with the family did not end, however, until 1913, and she continued to live with them in the palace.

Vicky's grandsons in 1885; Princes Wilhelm, in the Fauntleroy suit with the deep lace collar, Eitel Friedrich (right) and Adalbert of Prussia. The appointment of a nurse for these little princes caused a family argument – twice over. When Wilhelm was about to be born his grandmother expected to be asked to find a nurse. But her relationship with her eldest son was at a low ebb and he delighted in snubbing her; he consulted her sister Helena instead. Vicky was hurt and the Queen furious. 'I can't tell you how shocked and grieved I am at Willie's behaviour – which I have heard of from Lenchen. I strongly advised her to refuse to have anything to do with it'. But Helena did advise, choosing a 'good English nurse': two years later there was a renewed chorus of outrage from the older generation, including Helena, when the nurse she had chosen was sent away by the boys' parents – and replaced with a German. 'I think it very wrong of young people to pretend to know anything about the management of young children . . .', the Queen assured her daughter. 'Lenchen is very indignant and Christian too.'

Queen Victoria's first great-great-grandchildren, Princes Wilhelm (standing) and Louis Ferdinand of Prussia in the spring of 1908. In this generation too there were problems with a nurse. Wilhelm was a cheerful, confident baby but as time passed he became withdrawn and sullen. His grandmother could see that the nurse her daughter-in-law had chosen was too strict with him but she was afraid to intervene. Perhaps she was remembering all the trouble there had been when she had defied first Vicky and then Helena over nurses for her own children, and how unwilling she had been to take their advice. It was left to her husband to sort the problem out.

Little Alice of Albany, Leopold's daughter, was very fond of her nurse Mrs Creak, who was chosen by the Queen. But Mrs Creak could not get on with Charles Edward, Alice's brother, who was a nervous, difficult child. She favoured Alice, and eventually their mother decided that she must go, much to the Queen's annoyance.

One of the most famous royal nurse stories of all concerns Prince Edward (left) and Prince Albert of York, the Prince of Wales' grandsons, pictured here in 1897. In later years Edward described how his nurse had pinched him and twisted his arm before meetings with his parents so that he would scream and be sent away. The same nurse is said to have neglected his brother and the whole story has passed into folklore, with writers claiming that the cruelty lasted for three years without the parents noticing a thing. Some say that it was only discovered when the nurse had a nervous breakdown. All agree that the end came in 1897, when Mrs Charlotte Bill became head nurse. But the truth appears to have been rather different. There would have been several nurses in the York household but the head nurse when Edward was born was a Mrs Peters. She left in April 1897 to get married but continued to receive a pension for her time in service. Mrs Bill had already joined the household a year earlier: she told friends that she was appointed when the Duchess of York saw a nurse slap Prince Edward and dismissed her on the spot – this must have been one of the under nurses as Mrs Peters was still in position. Mrs Bill did not become head nurse herself until 1 July 1900.

Vicky was in England in January 1897. She adored small children and missed nothing, and it is very hard to believe that the children she described in a letter to her daughter Sophie were the victims of sustained cruelty: 'The eldest . . . is such a little love, and talks so plainly and is so forward. I think he is intelligent, he has a lovely compexion and such fair hair with dark blue eyes. He is a fascinating little child. The second is so bright and jolly and good-tempered and not a bit shy, not a pretty child exactly, though he has delightful little natural curls over his head, and the merriest of smiles. The little ones live quite close to me in the tower rooms, so I have a good opportunity of seeing them'.

Mrs Charlotte Bill with Princess Mary and Prince Henry in 1902.

Even the early cameras, with their long exposure times, could catch some delightfully informal moments. This photo, taken in 1867, shows Albert Victor, Louise and George of Wales.

Princesses Margarete (left) and Sophie of Prussia, Vicky's youngest daughters, with their father Crown Prince Friedrich, in August 1874.

Alice's grandsons Georg Donatus (left) and Ludwig of Hesse enjoying a game on the beach in 1910.

Arthur's daughter Daisy (Princess Margaret of Connaught) with her eldest son Gustav Adolf, Duke of Västerbotten. Daisy married the Hereditary Prince of Sweden in June 1905.

The Duchess of Albany, Leopold's widow, in 1910 with their grandchildren. Helen Albany was married to Leopold for barely two years. She mourned him for nearly forty, as the Queen did Prince Albert. Three of the six children grouped with her here belonged to her daughter and three to her son: they are, from the left, Prince Rupert of Teck (Alice's son), Princess Sibylla of Saxe-Coburg (Charlie's daughter), Prince Johann Leopold of Saxe-Coburg, Prince Maurice of Teck (Maurice died on a family visit to Coburg in September 1910 when he was six months old), Prince Hubertus of Saxe-Coburg and Princess May of Teck.

Alexandra, Princess of Wales, with her first grandchild Lady Alexandra Duff in 1891.

Princess Beatrice with her Spanish grandchildren Alfonso, Prince of the Asturias (left), Infanta Beatriz and Infante Jaime in 1911.

Sometimes appearances can be deceptive. This appealing little girl with her fur-trimmed velvet coat and muff is actually a little boy, Vicky's grandson Prince Adalbert of Prussia, in 1886.

This one really is a little girl; Princess Elisabeth of Hesse, Ernst Ludwig's daughter, in 1896.

Until after the First World War it was normal to dress small boys and girls in the same clothes. The dresses in these photographs are very similar but the seated child is a boy, Prince John of Wales, the youngest grandson of King Edward VII. The standing child is a girl, Princess Katherine of Greece, whose mother was Vicky's daughter Sophie.

The habit of dressing brothers and sisters alike also lingered. It would be possible to sort out this 1875 mixture of Hesse and Wales children on clothing alone: on the left, the child in the pale coat is Alix of Hesse-Darmstadt and the boy whose sailor suit doesn't quite match is her brother Ernst Ludwig. The others are Albert Victor, Victoria, Maud (sitting), George and Louise of Wales.

A generation later, in 1907, the same custom persists and sisters wear matching dresses. These are Affie's grandchildren: (l to r) Irma, Marie Melita, Gottfried and Alexandra of Hohenlohe-Langenburg – with two cats who look keen to escape.

Here too the elder of Princess Alice's great-granddaughters wear identical outfits: from the left, Theodora, Sophie (the baby), Margarita and Cecilie of Greece. Cecilie's dress is shaped slightly differently from her elder sisters' but trimmed to match.

Sometimes, even in royal circles, actual clothes were handed down. This photograph (right) is one of a popular series showing the Tsesarevich Alexei, Alice's grandson, wearing his first pair of trousers on his third birthday, in August 1907.

In 1909 Alexei's cousin Georg Donatus of Hesse (left) was photographed in the same suit, with its distinctive Russian-style tunic and patterned braiding. But the story does not end there. The birthday photographs of Alexei were published around the world and on 10 April 1909 the British magazine *Home Chat* advertised a pattern on its 'Children's Dress for Home Workers' page. 'The Percy Tunic' ('flat paper pattern sixpence-ha'penny; or tacked up, including flat, one shilling and three pence ha'penny') is an exact copy of Alexei's suit, even down to the zig-zag pattern on the braid. The child in the accompanying drawing has Alexei's long curls too – the Prince of Wales with his sailor suit was not the only infant trendsetter in the family!

National costume is a popular theme in the photographs of royal children: in this photo of around 1868 Alice's daughters Victoria (left) and Ella are dressed as Hessian peasants. A generation later a similar costume was made for their niece Elisabeth – it is still preserved at one of the family's homes.

In 1896 Affie's grandchildren Princess Elisabetha (left) and Prince Carol of Romania were photographed as Romanian peasants.

Two little Scandanavians: Arthur's grandsons Gustav Adolf and Sigvard of Sweden out sledging in around 1910 – though their costumes did serve a more practical purpose.

Another form of national costume worn by Queen Victoria's descendants whether they liked it or not during her lifetime was the kilt. Even German princes visiting Balmoral would be expected to play the part. This little Highlander is Helena's son, Albert of Schleswig-Holstein, in about 1873.

From the left, Leopold, Maurice and Alexander of Battenberg at Balmoral in 1894. Prince Maurice was born at Balmoral in 1891, and in honour of this unusual fact the name 'Donald' was added to his other names. The same thing happened to his elder sister, Victoria Eugenie Julia, which accounts for her final Christian name 'Ena'.

The most unlikely Highlanders of all; Vicky's grandsons Oskar and Joachim of Prussia with their sister Viktoria Luise, the youngest children of Prince Wilhelm who by this time (1895) had become Kaiser Wilhelm II. Prince Joachim's appearance is made even stranger by his long ringlets: Joachim was his mother's pet and, fancying him to be delicate, she clung to him far longer than his brothers.

Almost half a century after the little Prince of Wales wore his first sailor suit the idea had become universal. These children are also Vicky's grandsons: from the left, Wolfgang, Friedrich Wilhelm, Richard, Philipp, Christoph and Maximilian of Hesse-Cassel in 1901 – and it's interesting to note that the middle boys, both rising five, are still in skirts. This was an unusual family by any standards because their mother, Princess Margarete, produced six children with only four pregnancies: Philipp and Wolfgang, Christoph and Richard, were two sets of twins. When news of Margarete's first twin birth reached Balmoral, 'The Queen laughed very much and is rather amused at the list of her great grandchildren being added to in such a rapid manner' – however would she have reacted to the second pair?

Another 'English' sailor; Sophie of Prussia's youngest son Prince Paul of Greece, in about 1905.

In many of the Continental royal houses princes were given military rank at birth and put into uniform as soon as they could walk – sometimes before. Queen Victoria heartily disapproved of the custom so photographs of young British princes in uniform are rare, and where they do exist they are more likely to record acting or dressing-up costumes. This is one example, from about 1872, showing Prince Christian Victor of Schleswig-Holstein, Helena's eldest child, as a Scots Guard.

Games of soldiers, on the other hand, were enjoyed by little boys the world over. Here Prince Leopold of Battenberg emulates a trooper of the Household Cavalry. He seems to have been an endearing child. During a visit to Windsor in 1893 Vicky told her daughter, 'Little Leopold is my special favourite. "I love you, I do", he said to me yesterday, bringing me a bunch of white violets, "I picked them for you because I love you". Of course,' she added, rather sadly, 'I never get a chance of seeing my Berlin grandchildren, or knowing them, as I do these.' By 'the Berlin grandchildren' she meant Wilhelm's children, Wilhelm, Eitel Friedrich, Adalbert, August Wilhelm, Oskar, Joachim, and Viktoria Luise of Prussia.

Two little Swedish cavalrymen, Arthur's grandsons Gustav Adolf and Sigvard.

Princes John and George of Wales in 1908 with their cousin Olav, Crown Prince of Norway (right).

Prince Alexander Ferdinand of Prussia, only child of the Kaiser's fourth son Prince August Wilhelm, in 1914, his long curls looking very odd with full uniform.

5

Preparing for the World

After the nursery came the schoolroom, and the long preparation for adult life. In the first half of the nineteenth century the pattern followed was similar in all the European Courts. Princes were entrusted to a male governor, usually a soldier, and taught by a selected team of subject tutors — with their brothers if they had brothers, with a few hand-picked boys or alone if not. In the smaller Courts one tutor often had to provide all the lessons on his own. Royal education almost always included an element of military training — sometimes from the cradle. But as the nineteenth century progressed things did begin to change, with royal parents considering school as an option for their sons. For girls things were always simpler: they remained in the schoolroom with a governess until their confirmation. This was followed by the 'coming out', marriage and motherhood — or the often thankless existence of the maiden aunt.

Princes Edward and Albert of Wales on the scenic railway, their generation's equivalent of a theme park ride. Even in the most serious of households lessons were interrupted by outings and amusements. The dress is formal here and the expressions sombre, and the tutor looks more concerned to preserve good behaviour than to see that everyone has a good time. But Prince Albert, hiding his face behind his hand, appears to be excited – unless he was just avoiding the camera.

Albert (behind), George (in the kilt) and Henry of Wales with their tutor Mr Hansell in about 1910. The boys look more relaxed here and have probably interrupted a game for the photograph – Prince Henry is still holding the ball. Mr Hansell taught all George V's sons. An Oxford scholar and a keen sportsman, he believed that the princes would have been better in a school environment, but he did his best by making their surroundings and routine as much like school as possible. Edward and Albert went to the Royal Naval College at Osborne when they reached their teens while Henry and George were sent to St Peter's Court Preparatory School at Broadstairs in Kent. Henry went on from St Peter's Court to Eton and George to Osborne.

Prince Henry was the first son of a British sovereign to be sent to school. But the change began a generation earlier with his first cousin once removed, Prince Christian Victor of Schleswig-Holstein, seen here as Captain of the Wellington College cricket team in 1885. Christian Victor was the first British prince to attend school. In 1876 he was sent to a preparatory school near Bracknell in Berkshire, to be joined by his brother Albert three years later. In 1880 he went to Wellington College, a comparatively new public school in which his grandfather Prince Albert had taken great interest. 'I like the place very much,' Christian Victor wrote, 'there are some very nice boys here that I go out walks with. The work is not very hard. We have a Chemistry lesson twice a week.' Christian Victor was a keen cricketer. He was taught to play by the footman at Cumberland Lodge and organised regular games between boys from the Household and boys whose families worked on the Windsor Estate. From Wellington he went on to Oxford and the army.

Prince Maurice of Battenberg (right) in about 1902. Maurice and his brothers were taught at home by a Mr Theobald until the winter of 1903, when Princess Beatrice decided to spend six months in Egypt. She took Ena and her middle son Leopold, who suffered from haemophilia. Alexander had already entered the Navy and Maurice was sent to Locker's Park School at Hemel Hempstead in Hertfordshire, which he took to immediately. He was a lively, cheeky boy, full of energy and very friendly. At school they called him 'Plumpy'. In 1905 he went on to Wellington, then to Sandhurst.

Crown Prince Olav of Norway, grandson of King Edward VII, was born a prince of Denmark and christened Alexander. He changed his nationality and his name in 1905, when his father Prince Carl of Denmark was elected King of Norway. His mother was Princess Maud, youngest of the Wales sisters. Olav was educated privately at first but later went to a secondary school in Oslo: he is said to have been the first prince ever to attend an ordinary state school.

Prince Wilhelm of Prussia, the future Kaiser Wilhelm II and Vicky's eldest son, in about 1871. In the Prussian Court it was customary for a prince to be received into the army at the age of ten. Wilhelm was proud of his uniform but his mother deplored it, saying that he looked 'like some unfortunate little monkey dressed up, standing on the top of an organ.' It was partly to combat the effects of militarism on her elder sons that she wanted them to attend the Grammar School at Cassel, under the supervision of their tutor. Their grandfather Kaiser Wilhelm I was furious and there were many angry scenes before he would give way. But he did, and Wilhelm attended the school for three years. Afterwards he followed his father to Bonn University, but he remained unmoved by these centres of learning. He remembered the end of his education as a decisive moment: 'My longing from my earliest years was now satisfied: I could at last devote myself to the military life and to the great Prussian idea.'

The Kaiser's sons in 1900: (l to r standing) Eitel Friedrich, Wilhelm, Adalbert; (in front) Oskar, Joachim, August Wilhelm. Wilhelm's experience of Cassel made him something of an evangelist for a different form of education. His own sons, seen here in 1900, were steeped in Prussian tradition from childhood. Each was commissioned into the First Foot Guards on his tenth birthday and, at the age of twelve or thereabouts, sent on to the military cadet school at Plön where a house had been purchased for them, to segregate them from other pupils except those selected by their governor. Wilhelm relished the cadet schools and set out to re-model the German grammar schools in their image. He believed that too much emphasis on the Classics was bad for boys, because it denied them the chance to develop strong national feelings. He urged more detailed study of Germany and German history, less classroom work and more physical activity. His system would educate a number of Queen Victoria's descendants – and not all of them German.

Prince Waldemar (left) and Prince Sigismund of Prussia in full naval uniform, in about 1908. Wilhelm's brother Henry entered the developing German Navy rather than the army, and his sons seem to have followed his example. Waldemar, though, had inherited haemophilia and would have been unable to take part in any form of active service.

The Navy was also chosen for the sons of the Prince of Wales. Originally only Prince George (left) was picked for a naval cadet, but when the time came for him to join HMS *Britannia* at Dartmouth his tutor, the Rev. Dalton, advised against parting him from his older brother. Albert Victor's hearing was poor and this gave him a rather distant, dreamy air; his progress was already unremarkable and without the stimulus of his brother's company Dalton feared he would make no effort at all. The Queen did not see a naval training ship as any sort of preparation for the throne but eventually she gave way, and Albert Victor (right) joined his brother on *Britannia* for two years. Afterwards both boys served for three years on HMS *Bacchante*, cruising to Australia with Dalton on hand to supervise.

Prince Albert Victor in Hussar's uniform in 1885. After *Bacchante* Albert Victor was subjected to a period of intensive study before entering Trinity College Cambridge, in the autumn of 1883. His lazy good nature and easy-going temperament made him popular, but by no stretch of the imagination could he be called academic. He was not athletic either; hockey and tennis were his only active games. Still, he remained at Trinity for two years before leaving to join the army, and in 1885 he was commissioned in the 10th Hussars.

Prince George of Wales in 1884. George remained in the Navy, studied at the Royal Naval College, Greenwich and was appointed Sub Lieutenant at the age of nineteen.

Affie's grandson Prince Carol of Romania, seen here in about 1905 with his sisters Elisabetha (left) and Marie, was the subject of bitter and prolonged quarrels between his mother, Crown Princess Marie, and the Queen, her husband's aunt Queen Elisabeth of Romania (who, as Princess Elisabeth of Wied, had once been considered for marriage to the Prince of Wales – see p. 24). Marie was only seventeen when her son was born and Queen Elisabeth stepped in to organise the child's upbringing, appointing a nursery governess whom Marie came to hate so much that eventually she left for her parents' home, refusing to return until the woman was dismissed. The governess had come to represent everything that was wrong in the life of the unhappy young mother: sadly Carol, who was only six when the argument came to a head, was fond of the governess and did not want to lose her. A new governess was appointed and peace returned, but as he grew Carol became more wilful and difficult. His first tutor, chosen by the King, was a withdrawn and emotionally disturbed character who developed an unhealthy obsession with the boy. In this man's sole charge, Carol became increasingly withdrawn himself – yet even though the family could see the changes in him, the ordeal lasted until he was nearly grown up. Only then was the tutor dismissed. Carol was sent on to Potsdam for military training, in the hope that the hearty social atmosphere of a Prussian regiment would undo some of the damage that had been done.

Leopold's son Charles Edward, 2nd Duke of Albany, Duke of Saxe-Coburg-Gotha, as a member of the Borussia Corps of Bonn University in about 1904. The Borussia Corps was open only to students of the highest rank. Members spent their time drinking and fencing, and one of their proudest achievements was a duelling scar: in 1904 Charles Edward received a scar on the forehead. It was a strange position for a boy who began his schooldays in an English preparatory school and went on to Eton: Charles Edward was one of the victims of the Coburg succession, which became something of a poisoned chalice for Queen Victoria's family. Prince Alfred inherited Coburg from his uncle in 1893 though he was reluctant to move to Germany and stayed in the Navy until the very last moment. His only son, 'young Alfred', died in 1899. His brother Arthur was next in line but he refused the inheritance. Next came Arthur's son, Prince Arthur of Connaught. He was at Eton, and is said to have sought out his cousin Charles Edward, and threatened to beat him up if he did not take the title. Charlie was happy at Eton, but his widowed mother faced concerted pressure from her husband's family. She had no choice but to accept on his behalf. So, at the age of thirteen and speaking almost no German, Charlie was uprooted. At the Kaiser's suggestion he was sent to the Lichterfeld military academy at Potsdam and he went on from there to Bonn. He inherited the Coburg title a week after his sixteenth birthday.

Prince Wilhelm of Prussia, the future Kaiser, with his wife Auguste Viktoria and sons, from the left, Wilhelm, Eitel Friedrich and Adalbert, in 1885. After university and the army the next duty of a prince was to find a suitable bride. Wilhelm made his choice in 1878, proposing to Princess Auguste Viktoria of Schleswig-Holstein-Augustenburg, a niece of Prince Christian. Wilhelm was a strange and often contradictory character and his feelings for her wavered dramatically even during their long engagement; they were not married until 1881. But she performed her duty admirably, producing a long string of healthy princes and loyally supporting her husband for almost forty years. Her family worshipped her.

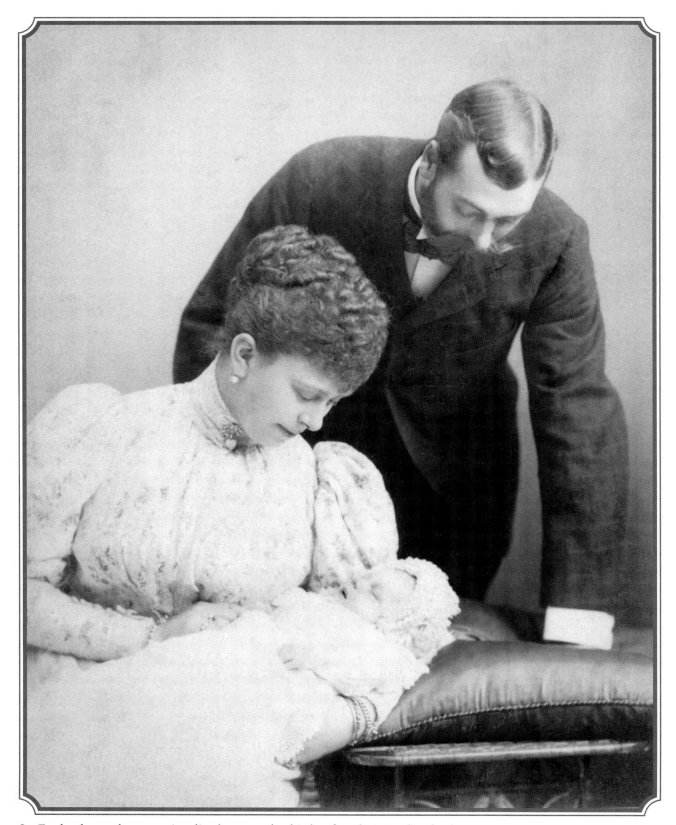

In England too the sovereign lived to see the birth of an heir in the third generation. Prince George married Princess May (Victoria Mary) of Teck in 1893 and is photographed here with his wife and first child, Prince Edward, born in the summer of 1894.

Victoria (centre), Elisabeth (right) and Irene of Hesse in about 1875. Marriage was still the best a princess could hope for, but ideas were changing. 'You say rightly, what a fault it is of parents to bring up their daughters with the main object of marrying them', Princess Alice assured her mother in 1874. 'I want to strive to bring up the girls without *seeking* this as the sole object for the future – to feel they can fill up their lives so well otherwise. . . . A marriage for the *sake* of marriage is surely the greatest mistake a woman can make.' Alice devoted a good deal of her time to educating her children herself, emphasising the importance of self-reliance and introducing them to her philanthropic work from an early age. As children, they also heard Brahms play piano duets with their mother and Jenny Lind sing, though sometimes the cultural level was pitched a little too high. After one nursery performance by the actress Frau Sonntag Princess Irene broke the silence with the simple verdict, 'That was ghastly!'

Arthur's daughters, Margaret and Patricia, 'Patsy', of Connaught, in about 1897–8. The Connaught sisters were educated at home, Bagshot Park in Surrey, by governesses. The Duchess of Connaught was a strict mother: the photographer Richard Speaight recalled an incident when the girls, bored by constant teasing, pushed their brother from the room and locked the door. There were several knocks which they ignored, shouting 'You can't come in until you have apologised.' 'All at once an expression of horror came over the faces of the princesses as they realized that it was not their brother who was trying to gain admittance. Panic-stricken, they moved to the door . . . the door opened, and the dignifiedly indignant figure of the Duchess of Connaught entered. I shall never forget her stately progress into the room, nor the swish of her train. Her expression froze me. . . . Neither the princesses nor myself had any chance to explain. I never saw the Duchess again.'

The Kaiser's only daughter, Princess Viktoria Luise of Prussia, seen here in 1908, was a tomboy, deeply envious of her six brothers and extremely spoilt, the youngest child in a close-knit and loving family. 'Her manners,' wrote her English governess Miss Topham, 'were astonishingly rude, and partook a good deal of "Papa's" bluffness. She had also a great sense of her own importance . . . Yet, with all her defects of character there was something likeable about her. She possessed generous and kindly impulses and was an ardent champion of the distressed . . . following the example of her mother the Empress – one of the kindest-hearted women I ever met.'

The confirmation of Princess Margaret of Connaught in the private chapel at Windsor Castle in March 1898. (The Windsor fire of 1992 began in the private chapel.) Margaret's parents, the Duke and Duchess of Connaught, with her sister Patricia and brother Arthur, can be seen on the left, facing the Queen and her daughters on the right, with Princess Beatrice and her daughter Ena closest to the camera. Confirmation traditionally marked the end of childhood, after which a girl would 'come out' and be considered for marriage.

Affie's children; Marie in front, holding her youngest sister Beatrice, 'Baby Bea', Victoria Melita (behind them), Alexandra and young Alfred (right), grouped around their cousin Prince George of Wales in 1891–2. George was very close to his Edinburgh cousins and hoped to marry Marie when she had reached the right age. In 1892 he spoke to her parents, but his offer was refused. It is said that the Duchess took this decision without even asking her daughter. In her Russian home marriages between first cousins were forbidden – besides, she had devoted time and effort to detaching her children from their English roots and teaching them to be German, in preparation for the day when their father would inherit the Coburg throne. But she did believe that a girl should be married young, before she had time to develop ideas of her own. A few weeks after George's proposal Marie became engaged to Crown Prince Ferdinand of Romania. She was just sixteen.

Princess Victoria of Prussia, one of the saddest of the Queen's granddaughters, in the early 1880s. Victoria was a gentle girl who thought only of marriage and babies – curiously her mother, Vicky, the most academic of the Queen's daughters, had brought up her daughters for marriage alone. Perhaps she sensed how out of place her own education had made her in her husband's country. Young Victoria would have fallen in love with any prince who offered, but she had the misfortune to fall for Prince Alexander of Battenberg. The Prussian establishment would not hear of marriage but her mother encouraged her to hope: the argument raged for years with Victoria left helpless on the sidelines, watching longingly as her cousins married and had babies. Eventually she became Princess Adolf of Schaumburg-Lippe, but she had no children. In later years, as a widow, she married a Russian refugee over thirty years younger than herself. He squandered her fortune and she was on the point of divorcing him when she died.

The Princess of Wales and her daughter Victoria (centre), celebrating the engagement of Princess Maud and Prince Carl of Denmark at Fredensborg in 1895. Maud also set her heart on the wrong man at first – Prince Francis of Teck, whom she had known from childhood. But she was happy with Carl, though she did not take to life in his Danish home and did not really settle until after 1905, when he became King of Norway.

In June 1905 King Alfonso XIII of Spain made a State visit to England. He was ready to marry and it was thought that he would propose to Patricia of Connaught, who had visited Spain the previous year. But she snubbed him, more than once, and by the end of the visit his eye was drawn to her cousin Ena of Battenberg, whose striking blond hair set her apart from the crowd. His mother did not like the idea but could not deter him, and in January 1906 the couple became engaged. Ena converted to Catholicism and they married in Madrid in May 1906. Queen Victoria always had deep misgivings about May weddings and this one certainly proved her case: an assassin's bomb thrown at the procession on its way back from the church killed several people and horses. When the couple arrived at the palace, Ena's wedding dress and train were heavily stained with blood.

Princess Irene of Hesse and Prince Henry of Prussia on their wedding day, 24 May 1888, at the chapel of the Charlottenburg Palace in Berlin. Queen Victoria was unhappy about this alliance of two of her grandchildren because it took place behind the backs of herself and Vicky at a time when their relationship with the rest of the Prussian royal family was at a low ebb. The wedding itself was a sad one. The old Kaiser, Wilhelm I, had died in March. His son Kaiser Friedrich III, 'Fritz', was also dying but determined to attend the service. Fritz's mother, the widowed Kaiserin Augusta, 'sat through the ceremony in a wheelchair like a black ghost.'

Princess Alice of Albany, Leopold's daughter, on the day of her wedding to Prince Alexander of Teck, 10 February 1904 – the 64th anniversary of the wedding of Queen Victoria and Prince Albert. The adult bridesmaids are Alice's cousins, Daisy (right) and Patsy of Connaught. The little girls are (from the left) Princess Mary of Wales, Princess Helen of Waldeck and Princess Mary of Teck.

Princess Alice of Battenberg with her husband Prince Andrew of Greece in Darmstadt in 1905. Their wedding in the Russian Chapel in Darmstadt in 1903 was the last of the great royal gatherings in the small German town, bringing together Russian, Greek, German and English cousins. As the couple left for their honeymoon the guests chased after the carriage through the streets in a mad scramble unthinkable at the more formal Courts. Tsar Nicholas II had several children clinging to his coat tails, and when he hurled his last bag of rice into the bride's carriage she hit him firmly over her head with her slipper, leaving him laughing in the road.

Princess Beatrice, 'Baby Bea' of Edinburgh and Saxe-Coburg and the Infante Alfonso of Spain on the right, about to leave for their honeymoon in July 1909, with, from the left, Prince Leopold of Battenberg, the Dowager Duchess of Saxe-Coburg and her third daughter Alexandra, Princess Ernst of Hohenlohe-Langenburg. The expressions may be severe, but the flower arrangements on the car are splendid.

Princess Marie of Edinburgh and Saxe-Coburg, Crown Princess of Romania, with her first child Prince Carol in 1894.

Vicky's youngest daughters, Sophie and Margarete of Prussia, with their husbands and children at Friedrichshof in 1904. Sophie is in the darker dress, standing beside her husband Constantine, Duke of Sparta. Margarete is on the right, next to her husband Friedrich Karl of Hesse-Cassel. The children are, from the left, George of Greece (standing), Philipp of Hesse-Cassel, Helen of Greece, Maximilian of Hesse-Cassel, Paul of Greece (behind, in a dress), Wolfgang of Hesse-Cassel directly in front of his elder brother Friedrich Wilhelm, Alexander of Greece in front of Richard of Hesse-Cassel, Christoph of Hesse-Cassel.

Alix of Hesse-Darmstadt as Tsaritsa Alexandra Feodorovna in 1898, with her daughters Olga (in the chair) and Tatiana. Alix held out against concerted pressure from the family, particularly her grandmother, to marry Albert Victor of Wales. 'She shows great strength of character', the Queen said, 'as all her family and all of us wish it and she refuses the greatest position there is.'

Victoria Melita of Edinburgh and Saxe-Coburg in 1909 with her children by her second husband, Grand Prince Kirill Vladimirovich of Russia; Maria (standing) and Kira. Divorce was rare in the early 1900s, but it did happen. Victoria Melita's first marriage to her cousin Ernst Ludwig of Hesse lasted seven years, ending in mutual unhappiness and leaving six-year-old Elisabeth, whose time had to be shared between her parents. Long before the marriage ended Victoria Melita had met a man she really loved, a cousin on her mother's side. Her decision to divorce Ernst Ludwig, and even more to marry Kirill, shocked the family on all sides.

Princess Victoria of Wales with her nephews, Edward, Albert and Henry of York in 1904. Like her aunt Beatrice before her, Victoria remained at home as her mother's companion. Many thought this selfish of Alexandra, though in later years she was pleased to see her daughter enjoy a platonic romance with one of the gentleman of the Court.

6

A Working Family

In a TV documentary about her working life, Queen Elizabeth II spoke of the importance of continuity at the heart of the monarchy: 'The King is dead, long live the King' – the seamless passing of the crown from generation to generation, with none of the uncertainties inherent in other systems. Simply by marrying and producing her nine children, Queen Victoria performed one of the principle duties of her office. Then, under Prince Albert's guidance, she established a tone of respectable domesticity which suited her country perfectly for decades. She also understood the importance of the great ceremonial occasions, much as she disliked them. The Queen was a hard-working woman, devoting herself to the duties of monarchy as she saw them throughout her long life and refusing to be swayed. Her adult children worked hard to extend the influence of monarchy into areas she could not or would not go: they established the pattern familiar to this day, visiting towns and villages around the country, opening institutions and public buildings and giving their names and support to a vast range of causes in the fields of medical and social reform, science and the arts. Two of the Queen's sons and four of her grandsons went on to became sovereigns in their own right. Five of her granddaughters became consorts to European sovereigns. Most of the others would work hard in whatever sphere was assigned to them – though not always with success.

The Queen at Coburg in 1894 with her daughter Vicky, the widowed Kaiserin Friedrich, sons Albert Edward, Prince of Wales (on the right), Alfred, Duke of Saxe-Coburg-Gotha (in the dark uniform) and Arthur, Duke of Connaught (on the left), and her grandson, Kaiser Wilhelm II. Groups like this emphasised a different sort of continuity: the sideways spread of the Queen's descendants into the European Courts.

Opposite: The Queen, her son Albert Edward, Prince of Wales, his son George, Duke of York and *his* son Prince Edward in about 1898. Simply to have the future of the throne secured into a fourth generation was an achievement unknown to previous monarchs, and photographs like this were extremely popular.

Princess Alix of Hesse (left), who became Tsaritsa of Russia in November 1894. She looks magnificent but also uncomfortable, as indeed she was, for Alix shared her grandmother's profound mistrust of high society. The glittering social life which had always characterised the Russian Court was alien to her nature; she eyed society with suspicion, they misunderstood her, and this breach would play a part in the final tragedy of imperial Russia.

Princess Marie of Edinburgh and Saxe–Coburg (right) as Crown Princess of Romania in the early 1900s. The photograph looks exaggerated to Western eyes. Marie was a flamboyant character and we assume that she is play-acting. To Romanians, however, images like this had great symbolic importance. Each element in the picture has a purpose. The costume evokes Romania's medieval past. The candelabra give a religious atmosphere, accentuated by the model church: in Orthodox imagery the ancient rulers often held models of the churches they had founded, and in other photographs from this series Marie is also shown holding the church. The photograph would have told ordinary Romanians that their future Queen was identifying herself with their past; she wanted to belong. Marie's husband Ferdinand did not become King until 1914. It was wartime. There could be no coronation until 1922, but when it happened Marie designed the costumes, and chose for herself a high crown similar to this. The Coronation stamps also showed her in this costume. Flamboyant she may have been, but she knew how to use her dramatic flair to enhance her position.

Princess Maud of Wales, Queen Maud of Norway, in the early 1900s. Maud took to being Queen exceptionally well, though she was surprised and amused by the sudden change in her fortunes – after all, she had only married a younger son with a junior role in his own country. She was very shy by nature but mastered the Norwegian language and looked out for causes that could benefit from royal patronage, showing a surprising lack of prejudice. Eyebrows were raised in 1907 when she advocated support for unmarried mothers, but she was not deterred and her health, which had always been very poor, seemed to improve in response to the challenge of her position.

Princess Ena of Battenberg, Queen Victoria Eugenie of Spain, looking every inch the Queen but strained and unhappy, which is a fair reflection of the truth. Ena's coolness and reserve was not at all understood in Spain. Like her cousin Alix, she had the wrong temperament for her country of adoption. But unlike Alix, she lacked even the consolation of a happy marriage: Alfonso's ardour waned very quickly and he blamed her for the tragic inheritance of haemophilia in his eldest and youngest sons. He took little trouble to hide his unfaithfulness, though they remained together for form's sake until after they were forced to leave the country in 1931.

Princess Sophie of Prussia, Queen of the Hellenes. For twenty-four relatively peaceful years – for herself, if not for Greece – Sophie was simply wife of the heir to the throne. She brought up her six children and devoted herself to her new country, involving herself in a range of social and educational causes. When there was war in the Balkans she founded her own hospital. Her title and circumstances changed when her father-in-law King George I was murdered, ushering in a long series of troubles for the family.

King Edward VII and Queen Alexandra on the day of their Coronation, 9 August 1902. 'Bertie' was heir to the throne longer than any other prince in British history. He must have wondered if the moment would ever come, but over the years he had carved out for himself a significant role in public affairs and had established contacts in Britain and on the Continent which would be valuable once he was King. He had played hard, but he worked hard too: his style and skills were very different from those of his mother but he made an effective monarch, with a real flair for the human side of the role.

The Coronation of King Haakon VII and Queen Maud of Norway at Trondheim on 22 June 1906. For some of the older generation the idea that a prince could be elected King was too much. Queen Victoria's cousin, the Grand Duchess of Mecklenburg Strelitz was outspoken on the subject; 'A *revolutionary* Coronation! such a *farce*,' she told her niece, the Duchess of York, '*I don't like your being there for it, it looks like sanctioning* all that nasty Revolution.'

The Coronation of King Ferdinand and Queen Marie of Romania at Alba Julia in Transylvania on 15 October 1922. There was no historical tradition of coronations in Romania. A church was specially built for the religious service that preceded Ferdinand's coronation: the ceremony itself took place in the town square. The Queen arranged the ceremony and designed the costumes. Her crown was based on a fresco of the legendary Princess Despina Doamna at Curtea de Arges.

King George V and Queen Mary at the Delhi Durbar on 12 December 1911, held to celebrate the King's accession. There had been earlier Durbars, in 1877 and 1903, but nothing on this scale had ever been seen, or would ever be seen again. The King himself suggested that he should go to Delhi and his Ministers at first were uneasy: no English monarch had visited the East since Richard I. To his mother the King wrote, 'The Durbar yesterday was the most wonderful & beautiful sight I have ever seen & one I shall remember all my life'.

King George V and Queen Mary presenting their eldest son Prince Edward to the crowds after his investiture as Prince of Wales at Caernarvon Castle on 13 July 1911. This was another of the great public events attended by some ten thousand people, but the hero of the hour was not happy. It was the specially designed costume that upset him, 'what would my Navy friends say if they saw me in this preposterous rig?' There was an argument but his mother assured him, 'Your friends will understand that as a Prince you are obliged to do certain things that may seem a little silly. It will be only for this once.'

Edward as King, saluting, riding to the Trooping of the Colour in 1936 supported by his three brothers; (from the left) Prince Albert, Duke of York, Prince Henry, Duke of Gloucester, Prince George, Duke of Kent.

Prince Albert of Schleswig-Holstein (second left) with Count Zeppelin (centre) and Kaiser Wilhelm II (second right) on board the Kaiser's yacht in the early 1900s. Albert would have preferred not to be under the Kaiser's wing, but royal duty often had to come before private plans. Unlike his brother Christian Victor, Albert had no wish to be a soldier. He went to Charterhouse School, but was forced to abandon whatever hopes he may have had and go to Germany, to be groomed as heir to his childless cousin Ernst Günther. Military training at Potsdam was inescapable. 'Poor Abby came to luncheon yesterday', the Queen told her daughter. 'He is miserable and says he hates the sight of a soldier and can't bear being on horseback and is to go into a cavalry regiment. A fine look out! I dread a failure.'

The Duke and Duchess of York with their son Prince Edward on board HMS *Crescent* in about 1897. The original printed caption on the mount of the photograph reads 'Cruise of H.M.S. *Crescent* commanded by Captain H.R.H. the Duke of York.'

Grand Princess Tatiana Nikolaievna (above), granddaughter of Princess Alice, as Commander-in-Chief of the 8th Vosnesensky Lancers, outside the Alexander Palace at Tsarskoe Selo, *c.* 1913. It was not only princes who had military duties; many of their sisters had them too, and enjoyed them. Tatiana's ankle-length dark green uniform with its bright yellow facings, collar and piping, and impossibly slim waist, survives to this day.

Princess Viktoria Luise of Prussia as Chief of the 2nd Guards Hussars Regiment in 1909–10. The Kaiser appointed his daughter Chief of the 'Death's Head' Hussars a few days after her confirmation and she was delighted. 'I can never thank you enough', she told him, 'I have always regretted not having been a boy, so as to be able to join your army'.

For some princes public duties started very young. The baby is Prince Michael of Romania making his first public appearance at an official function, a military parade in held Bucharest in honour of a visiting Japanese prince in the spring of 1924. In the centre is Michael's mother Helen, Queen Sophie of the Hellenes' daughter, looking rather awkward and out of place and showing, perhaps, why the crowds found her less sympathetic than her more outgoing mother-in-law Queen Marie, who stands beside her. On the left is Marie's youngest daughter Ileana. The lady holding Michael, his nurse Miss St John, was formerly nurse to the Greek royal family.

Charles Edward of Saxe-Coburg's children Hubertus (left), Sibylla and Johann Leopold, with their mother Duchess Victoria Adelheid. Carriage processions were the first experience of public life for many royal children: Ernst Ludwig of Hesse's younger son Ludwig recalled this as his earliest memory; Charles Edward felt sick during the procession for his grandmother's Diamond Jubilee and had to be transferred to a St John's ambulance, and George V's children had a fight in their carriage on the way back from the 1910 Coronation.

The Russian imperial children on parade; Tsesarevich Alexei and his sisters, from the left, Marie, Tatiana, Anastasia and Olga, in Court dress in about 1910.

Edward, Prince of Wales and his aunt, Queen Maud of Norway, riding in the Silver Jubilee procession of 1935.

Tsar Nicholas II and his family visiting the Peschersky Lavra in Kiev in 1911. The Tsar walks in front with the cleric, presumably the abbot; behind them the Tsaritsa Alexandra with Alexei, Tatiana on the right and Olga behind her brother; Maria can be seen behind her mother's shoulder and Anastasia only by her skirt, shoulder and the edge of her hat. The young man in uniform walking behind her is Crown Prince Boris of Bulgaria.

In the aftermath of the Russian Revolution the smaller countries to the west of the new Soviet state felt threatened by their huge neighbour and joined in 1921 in a defensive alliance. Marshal Pilsudski, the President of Poland, made a State visit to Romania in 1922 which sealed the treaty the two countries had signed; he appears here on the balcony at Foisor, the country home of the Crown Prince and Princess of Romania at Sinaia, in September 1922. The photo shows, from the left, King Ferdinand, Crown Princess Helen, Queen Marie, Crown Prince Carol, Marshal Pilsudski, Princess Irene of Greece (the Crown Princess's sister), Prince Nicholas of Romania. In 1924 King Ferdinand and Queen Marie made a return visit, and the friendship between the two countries developed to such an extent that there was even a move to make Prince Nicholas King of Poland. Nothing came of this, but there was a further Polish State visit to Romania in 1936, and in 1937 Carol, as King Carol II, visited Warsaw with his son Michael. On the outbreak of war in 1939 the Polish government was allowed to cross Romanian territory despite German protests, taking its armed forces and the country's gold reserves to assist the Allies.

From the left, in front, Elizabeth, Duchess of York, Crown Prince Carol of Romania and Prince Albert, Duke of York in Belgrade during the wedding celebrations of Prince Paul of Serbia and Princess Olga of Greece, on 22 October 1923. Behind are the Crown Prince's sister Ileana (right), the Crown Princess (between her husband and the Duchess of York), and other members of the family. The Duke and Duchess had been despatched abruptly to Belgrade by the Foreign Office, interrupting a peaceful holiday in Norfolk. It was a double celebration; on 21 October they attended the christening of Crown Prince Peter of Yugoslavia. The Duke was godfather and his quick reactions proved critical when the Patriarch accidentally dropped the naked six-week-old baby into the font. The Duke rescued him, though the rest of the service was drowned out by Peter's outraged screaming.

Queen Victoria at her desk, assisted by her servant Abdul Karim, the 'Munshi'. Victoria excelled at the unseen work of monarchy – the desk job. She was a prolific writer of letters and memoranda, building up a network of contacts across Europe and developing a shrewd understanding of international affairs.

The Prince and Princess of Wales, captured on camera during a visit to Glasgow in the 1890s. Civic visits, openings, loyal addresses and dedications helped to increase the popularity and prestige of the monarchy, and they were the Prince's great strength. Denied access to official papers by his mother, he had a real flair for public events.

Grand Duke Ernst Ludwig of Hesse-Darmstadt in the early 1900s. The arts also benefited from royal patronage, and nowhere more so than in the small state of Hesse and by Rhine. Ernst Ludwig was young and inexperienced when his father died, but full of plans for the future. Drawing inspiration from an idea of his mother's, inspired in turn by John Ruskin, a close friend of her brother Leopold, Ernst Ludwig set aside an area of land in Darmstadt as the setting for an artists' colony. He invited young artists working in the style of the day – Art Nouveau – to set up home, designing and building their own houses, studios and workshops. Exhibitions were held, in the hope that as time passed the artists' colony would become a resource for the whole state of Hesse, providing good designs for all areas of manufacture and building. The Grand Duke was also an enthusiast for garden design: his hopes did not all bear fruit but his encouragement of the arts has left its distinctive mark in Darmstadt and other Hessian towns.

Die drei Präsidentinnen des Alice-Frauenvereins-für Krankenpflege im Großherzogtum Hessen

Hanns Pellar

A picture postcard image celebrating the work of three royal ladies, also in Hesse, 'the three Presidents of the Alice-Frauenvereins for Nursing in the Grand Duchy of Hesse'. Princess Alice, in the centre, established the Frauenvereins (women's societies) with the idea of organising and training women to perform relief work in wartime, particularly nursing. The idea grew and spread, taking everyday nursing into consideration, the care of orphans, the mentally ill, nursing mothers, and the general employment and welfare of women. Alice achieved an astonishing amount in her short life. After her death her eldest daughter Victoria (right) gradually took over her position at the centre of the Frauenvereins. Ernst Ludwig's first wife, Victoria Melita, took no interest in Hesse and its affairs so Victoria held the position until her brother married for a second time. His new wife Eleonore (left) was as inventive and energetic in a good cause as he was, and immensely capable. She took over the Presidency, adding refinements of her own, particularly in the sphere of fund raising. She used the sale of postcards, usually private photos of her family, to raise money, organising 'postcard weeks'. During the postcard week of 1912 she arranged Germany's first ever air mail delivery: the flight of the aeroplane *Yellow Dog* on 10 June, carrying sacks of special postcards, was cheered by an enthusiastic crowd.

One of Grand Duchess Eleonore's charity postcards, sold for the 'Eleonorenheim', her orphanage, in 1915. The photo shows the Grand Duchess at home with her sons, Georg Donatus, left, and Ludwig.

'A Souvenir of the Royal Visit to South Staffordshire, Aug. 3rd 1909: The Nurses' Home at Tipton, opened by Princess Aribert (the King's Niece).' Alice was not the only royal lady to take an interest in nursing: her sister Helena was active in this country and her daughters continued her work. Princess Aribert was the married name of Helena's daughter Marie Louise, which she continued to use even though her marriage to Prince Aribert of Anhalt had ended in divorce. Small-scale visits like this, to a building that looks little more than a modest house – in an area unused to royal visitors where it was necessary to explain who the Princess was – were as important as major events in raising morale and making people feel that their good work had been noticed.

Queen Ena of Spain in Red Cross Uniform, in about 1916. Queen Ena faced an uphill struggle in her attempts to introduce welfare work in Spain. Her awareness of poor conditions was viewed as criticism, even in a country where general medical services were hopelessly backward. It was still seen as shameful in Spain for any woman other than a nun to go near a sick man: the country had no trained nurses at all. Ena began by organising lotteries to raise money to build hospitals and establish nursing training. In 1916 she founded the Spanish Red Cross under her personal direction. She was also President of the Anti-Tuberculosis League and her efforts were tireless. As people began to see the benefit – and the need – the movement gained momentum, though in later years the importance of Ena's pioneering role would often be overlooked.

Princess Mary, Queen Victoria's great-granddaughter, continuing the good work into the next generation with a visit to the Sussex County Hospital at Brighton on 22 November 1921.

7

Illness and Death

Death and grief are an inevitable part of family life. Illness too. Queen Victoria passed many admirable qualities to her descendants but the saddest aspect of her legacy, and the one she could do nothing about, was the haemophilia inherited by her male descendants. It is doubtful if she even understood that the condition came through her: perhaps it was better that way. It seems most likely now that the Queen inherited the defective gene from her mother and she from hers and so on, back through generations of women. There is an unusually high incidence of the loss of sons in the Queen's female line ancestry stretching back to the seventeenth century. A haemophilia sufferer's blood lacks the ability to clot properly. Any injury, particularly internal injury, is dangerous, many routine illnesses bring on bleeding, and everyday symptoms include pain and swelling around the joints. As if this were not problem enough, in recent years it has also been suggested that porphyria was present among the Queen's descendants. Porphyria is a hereditary disorder affecting the actual chemistry of the blood and giving rise to all manner of symptoms – or no symptoms at all. It was responsible for the apparent madness of Victoria's grandfather, King George III.

Royal haemophilia is certain, porphyria less so, but the family also shared the everyday illnesses and dangers of their time. There were tragedies, and royal death is usually a public event, with public rituals to be observed.

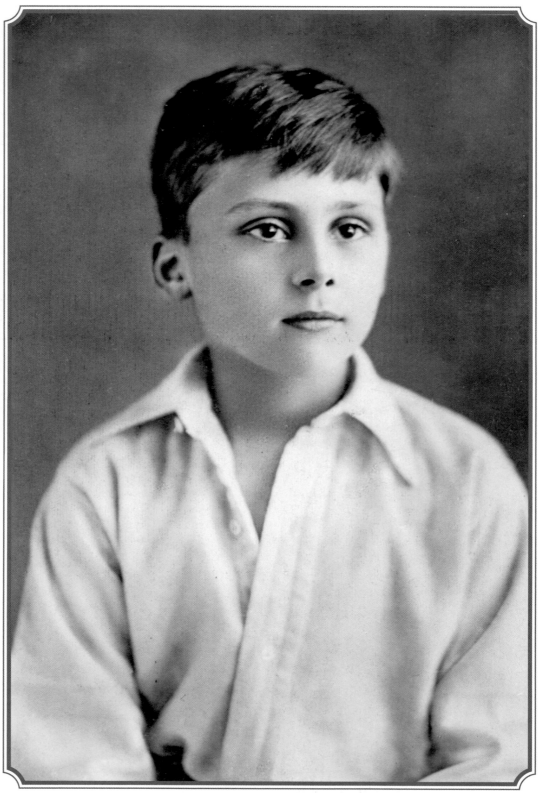

Prince Rupert of Teck, Leopold's grandson, *c.* 1919. As a haemophilia sufferer, Leopold could not avoid passing the gene to his daughter Alice. Rupert was her elder son, and he died in hospital in France following a car crash. He was not quite twenty-one. His younger brother Maurice, who died in infancy, may also have been haemophilic.

The second sufferer in the royal family was the elder Princess Alice's son 'Frittie' (Friedrich Wilhelm) of Hesse-Darmstadt. Ironically he was Leopold's godson. His condition was not recognised until he was two: a few months later, on a morning in May 1873, he was playing with his brother Ernst Ludwig in their mother's room, waving to one another from facing windows at an angle of the palace, when his chair toppled over and he fell out onto the balcony below. It was no great distance but he never regained consciousness and died later in the day. The photograph was taken in April, a few weeks before the accident happened.

Prince Leopold of Battenberg, Princess Beatrice's middle son, was also haemophilic, though his two brothers were healthy. He suffered particularly with his legs: frequent attacks had made him lame and he often appears in photographs with a stick; sometimes in a wheelchair. In April 1922 he needed an emergency operation at Kensington Palace and he died the next day.

Prince Waldemar of Prussia with his father Prince Henry at Balmoral in the 1890s. Waldemar was Frittie's nephew, the elder son of Irene of Hesse. His younger brother Heinrich was also haemophilic and died at the age of four, but Waldemar was a survivor. Though his health was precarious and he often came close to death, he managed to reach the age of fifty-six. He was taken ill in the closing months of the Second World War while trying to escape the advancing Soviet Army, and died because the clinic where he was taken could not perform blood transfusions.

Tsesarevich Alexei of Russia in 1913. The most famous haemophilia sufferer of all, Alexei was Frittie's nephew and a first cousin of Waldemar and Heinrich. He was born a few months after Heinrich's death and his haemophilia was discovered almost at once, when he began to bleed from the naval. His parents could do nothing but watch, trying to give him as normal a life as possible and keeping the truth hidden from everyone outside their immediate circle. Alexei was a lively, perceptive boy with great strength of character. His father's decision to abdicate for him in 1917 because of his condition was understandable, but it may have cost the dynasty and the family their only chance of survival.

The sons of Queen Ena and King Alfonso: (l to r) Infante Gonzalo, Alfonso, Prince of the Asturias, Infante Juan and Infante Jaime. In Spain too haemophilia was more than a private tragedy. Ena inherited the gene from her mother Princess Beatrice and passed it to two of her sons, the eldest, Alfonso, and the youngest, Gonzalo. Circumcision was customary in the Spanish royal family so the diagnosis was made soon after birth. The King never forgave Ena and never came to terms with what had happened. To make matters worse, the Infante Jaime suffered double mastoiditis at the age of four and the resulting operation left him deaf; his speech never developed properly. The Prince of the Asturias renounced his rights to the throne to marry a commoner: he died in a car crash in 1938. Gonzalo had already been killed on the road in Austria four years earlier.

Princess Charlotte of Prussia, Vicky's eldest daughter, with her daughter Feodora in 1880. Charlotte married Prince Bernhard of Saxe-Meiningen in 1878 and Feodora was their only child. Medical records demonstrate conclusively that both Charlotte and Feodora suffered from porphyria; the case for its having been inherited through Queen Victoria is less clear-cut.

The children of George V and Queen Mary in about 1916: (l to r behind) Prince Albert, Prince Edward, Prince Henry; (in front) Prince John, Princess Mary, Prince George. Prince John has attracted much attention in recent years. He was born in 1904 and developed epilepsy at the age of four. John lived a normal, probably rather pampered life as the youngest child in the family and there are endless stories of his mischief. Children who played with the young princes at Balmoral wondered why John had to be roped to his nurse when climbing in the hills and Theodore Roosevelt, after a visit to England in 1911, described John as a cheeky boy who irritated the King by dropping his 'h's – a habit picked up from his nurse. But his epilepsy worsened and the doctors advised that he would not live long. In 1917, with Princes George and Henry at school and the rest of the family engaged in war work, John was settled at Wood Farm on the Sandringham Estate with Mrs Bill, who had nursed him all his life. The family visited when they could and wrote regularly and his grandmother, Queen Alexandra, was nearby in Sandringham House. It was a caring environment: John had his own garden and toys and was taken on outings. He died at Wood Farm on 18 January 1919.

Prince Sigismund of Prussia, Vicky's third son, in November 1865. The Austro-Prussian war was at its height and his father away fighting when Sigismund was taken ill. He had meningitis. His mother never really overcame her grief at his death. 'Sigismund is the greatest darling I have ever seen', his aunt Alice had written only a few months earlier, 'so wonderfully strong and advanced for his age – with such fine colour, always laughing and so lively he nearly jumps out of our arms.'

Princess Alice, holding her youngest daughter 'May' in 1877 with (l to r) Ella, Alix, Victoria, Ernst Ludwig and Irene. Louis of Hesse succeeded his uncle as Grand Duke of Hesse and by Rhine in June 1877. After a hard-working year, the following summer the couple brought their children to England, spending several weeks in Eastbourne and returning to Darmstadt in the autumn. On 8 November Princess Victoria began to feel pain in her throat and neck. Her mother thought it might be mumps but it was diphtheria, and as the days passed the other children fell ill in turn, all except Ella, who was sent to her grandmother's. On 15 November the Grand Duke himself became ill and the next day Princess May died. Alice had to endure the funeral alone and she continued to nurse the rest of the family until 8 December, when she came down with diphtheria herself. She was too exhausted to resist and on 14 December, the seventeenth anniversary of her father's death, she died.

Prince Waldemar of Prussia, Vicky's youngest son, in the mid-1870s. Waldemar also succumbed to diphtheria only three months after his aunt Alice. 'Although rather more spirited than is easy to manage,' his mother had told the Queen only a month before, 'he is so trustworthy and honest and has such an open, fine, manly disposition. I shall feel it dreadfully when he goes to school, as he is my very own boy.'

Kaiser Friedrich III, 'Fritz', fought a long and painful battle against cancer of the throat. After thirty years as a political outcast, cold-shouldered by the ruling elite of his own country, he came to the throne in March 1888 as a dying man and reigned only ninety-eight days.

Prince Albert Victor with his fiancée Princess May of Teck in 1891. Albert Victor did not distinguish himself particularly in any phase of his career, but he was gentle, polite and kind-hearted. The Queen liked him best of her grandsons: the lethargy and lack of spirit that was so apparent to other men probably made him a more congenial companion as far as she was concerned. She disliked male heartiness and her husband had also been a quiet man. Her aim had been for Albert Victor to marry Alix of Hesse-Darmstadt, her favourite granddaughter. When that fell through, and the attempt to arrange a marriage with the Catholic princess of his choice, Hélène of Orleans had also come to nothing, the Queen was happy to nudge him in the direction of an English cousin, Princess May of Teck, who had known him from childhood. They became engaged in December 1891. Early in the New Year of 1892 Albert Victor contracted influenza at a family funeral. Pneumonia followed, and he died at Sandringham on 14 January.

Princess Elisabeth of Hesse-Darmstadt in 1901. Elisabeth was an engaging, wistful child who suffered acutely from her parents' divorce. Her father adored her. Miss Eagar, who nursed the Tsar's four daughters, wrote, 'Looking at her I used to wonder what those wide grey-blue eyes saw, to bring such a look of sadness'. In the autumn of 1903 Elisabeth died of typhoid while she and her father were staying with the Tsar's family: her body was taken back to Darmstadt in a silver coffin given by the Tsar and her father arranged a white funeral, with white instead of black for the funeral trappings, white flowers, and white horses for the procession.

Prince Mircea of Romania in 1915. Mircea was Marie of Romania's youngest child. He also died of typhoid in the autumn of 1916, with enemy troops advancing across the country and chaos all round. Soon afterwards his family was forced to evacuate the palace and they could not return for two years.

Tsaritsa Alexandra Feodorovna with her daughters in 1913; from the left, Grand Princesses Olga, Tatiana, Anastasia and Maria. Violent death was unheard of in Queen Victoria's family before the First World War, though she and her elder sons survived assassination attempts. But in Russia things were different. The Queen's grandson-in-law Grand Prince Sergei Alexandrovich was assassinated in Moscow in 1905. Alix and her husband, Tsar Nicholas II, their four daughters and only son, the Tsesarevich Alexei, were murdered by the Bolsheviks in Ekaterinburg on 17 July 1918. On 20 August 2000 they were canonised by the Russian Orthodox Church.

ZUR ERINNERUNG

an unseren

Erbprinzen Alfred v. S. C.-G.

geb. d. 15. October 1874
gest. d. 6. Februar 1899.

Verlag von Aug. Hermann, Hoflieferant, Coburg.

Mourning card for Prince Alfred of Saxe-Coburg-Gotha, Affie's only son. Behind the official face of grief lies one of the tragedies of the Coburg succession. In 1883, at eight years old, young Alfred was moved to Coburg to be educated as a German prince and future ruler. With his family miles away except in the holidays, he was entrusted to a right-wing German nationalist tutor who was charming to adults but overbearing with his pupil, constantly ridiculing him in front of others. It was no wonder that once Alfred outgrew this he ran wild, sampling all the temptations that life in a Prussian Guards regiment could offer. By 1892 he had contracted venereal disease. In 1898 he was dismissed from his regiment and by the New Year he was too ill to walk properly and his speech was becoming incoherent. Still his parents refused to believe that his state was critical. They celebrated their Silver Wedding at the end of January with Alfred lying ill downstairs, then sent him to a sanatorium at Meran in the Tyrol: he died soon after of 'paralysis of the larynx caused by the state of the brain.' Officially it was tuberculosis. Not surprisingly there were rumours: many believe to this day that he had shot himself, perhaps after contracting a secret marriage which his parents did not approve, but it seems unlikely. The illness alone was enough to account for his death.

The funeral of King Alexander of Yugoslavia in Belgrade: the new King, eleven-year-old Peter, stands in the front beside his mother Queen Marie (Marie of Romania's second daughter), draped from head to foot in black. Behind are the Regent, Prince Paul of Yugoslavia and his wife Olga, behind them is Peter's uncle King Carol II of Romania (in a peaked cap, looking upwards), and behind him Prince Nicholas of Greece, Prince George, Duke of Kent, and Prince Kirill of Bulgaria. King Alexander was shot in the streets of Marseilles on 9 October 1934, during a State visit to France.

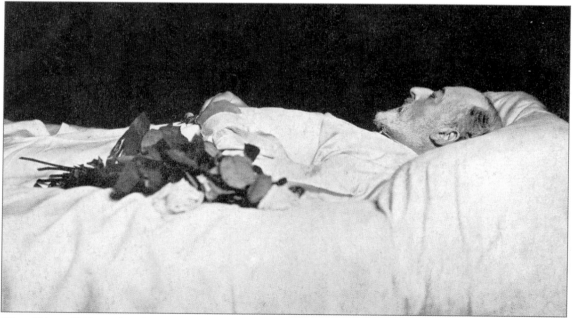

King Edward VII on his death bed in May 1910. Death-bed photographs of royalty were common on the Continent but almost unknown in this country. But Queen Alexandra, being Danish, did not share British sensibilities and was happy not only to have photographs taken of her husband, but also to have them published.

King Edward VII's lying-in-state in Buckingham Palace: an essential part of the ritual that surrounds royal deaths.

The new King, George V, and his sons Edward (close to the camera) and Albert walk behind the King's coffin in the funeral procession.

The custom is universal. This photo of the funeral of Crown Princess Margaret of Sweden, Daisy of Connaught, who died suddenly when infection set in following a mastoid operation, was taken on 13 May 1920. It shows the coffin followed through the streets by the widowed Crown Prince Gustav Adolf and his four eldest children; from the left, Gustav Adolf, Ingrid, Bertil and Sigvard.

The funeral of Queen Marie of Romania in 1938 with her children; Ileana (on the extreme left, looking down), Elisabetha, Nicolas and Carol.

Opposite: Grand Duke Ernst Ludwig of Hesse died peacefully in October 1937, and although he had not reigned in Hesse for nearly twenty years he received what amounted to a State funeral. His sons followed the coffin through the streets of Darmstadt to the Rosenhöhe, the traditional burial place of the Hesse family. Here the widowed Grand Duchess Eleonore and her sons, Ludwig (in front) and Georg Donatus, wait on the steps of the mausoleum.

Just a few weeks after the funeral, on 16 November 1937, Eleonore, Georg Donatus, his wife Princess Cecilie of Greece and their two young sons, with the children's nurse and a family friend, left for England, where Prince Ludwig was due to be married. They chose to fly, but the aeroplane hit a factory chimney near Ostende and crashed in flames, killing all those on board. The wedding took place in private the next day at St Peter's Church, Eaton Square; then the couple returned to visit the crash site and accompany the bodies home. The funeral took place in Darmstadt on 19 November, with a five-mile procession through the streets. Prince Ludwig, as chief mourner, walks in front, then (from the left, first row) Prince Gottfried of Hohenlohe-Langenburg, Princes Christoph and Philipp of Hesse-Cassel, Prince Philip of Greece (now the Duke of Edinburgh) and Prince Berthold of Baden. Lord Mountbatten is in the row behind, in the distinctive naval hat, to the right of him is Prince August Wilhelm of Prussia.

From the left, Princess Maud, the Princess of Wales, Prince George and Princess Victoria, in mourning for Prince Albert Victor, 1892. Mourning was always worn after a death, for set periods; two years for a husband, twelve months for a parent or child, four to six months for a brother or sister, and so on. These customs relaxed slightly after 1900, but long into the century black was still worn as a matter of form and many widows wore it for life.

The Queen with Princess Ena of Battenberg in 1896. Their mourning here is for Prince Henry of Battenberg, Ena's father. He did much to enliven the Queen's latter years but felt confined by her routines; in 1895 he asked to join an expeditionary force to Ashanti in western Africa. There was no fighting, but he contracted malaria and died on board HMS *Blonde* off the African coast on 20 January 1896.

Princess Louise, the Princess Royal and Duchess of Fife, with her daughters Alexandra (standing) and Maud in 1912. The Fifes were sailing to Egypt in December 1911 when their ship, the P & O liner *Delhi*, hit a sandbank off Cape Trafalgar. The Fifes were among the last to leave the ship, and the ship's boat on which they were taken was swamped several times by the waves; Princess Alexandra was washed over but a young engineer clung to her hand. Maud was also washed over closer to shore, and once all the passengers had struggled to the beach they had a five-mile walk to find shelter. After some weeks' rest they went on to Egypt, but the Duke had developed a cough and fever. Pleurisy set in and he died at Aswan on 29 January.

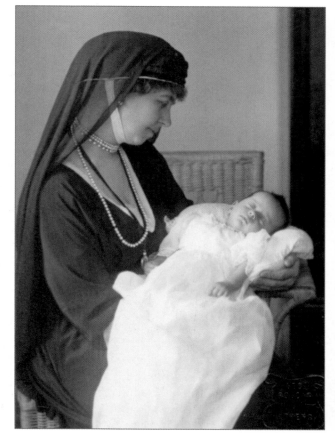

Queen Sophie of the Hellenes holding her granddaughter Alexandra in 1921. The Queen wears mourning here for her son Alexander, the baby's father, who died five months before his child was born. The curious head dress, similar to a nun's habit, became a fashionable part of mourning wear in the 1920s.

War in the Family

Queen Victoria's family was part of a wider international family of royalty. Most of its members conversed fluently in two, three or even four languages and all enjoyed a network of family relationships across Europe, which became more complex with each generation. Once it was thought that this very complexity would help to secure peace in Europe, but when war came the family suffered the added pain of separation from their brothers, sisters, parents on the other side of the lines. They also shared the responsibilities of their own country at war: fighting, for most of the princes, nursing and morale-boosting at home for their mothers and sisters and the older men – sometimes for the children too. The Queen's family was involved in several wars during the nineteenth century, in Europe and across the Empire, but the First World War of 1914–18 cut across all their lives, ending the comfortable certainties of the old world.

The first members of the Queen's family to face the divisive effects of war were her elder daughters Alice (left) and Vicky, seen here in the mid-1860s. When the German countries declared war in 1866, with Prussia facing Austria and the smaller states compelled to choose between them, the sisters found themselves on opposing sides: Vicky's husband commanded one of the three Prussian armies in the field while Alice's husband was a front line officer in the Hessian regiments, fighting for Austria. While Vicky became progressively excited by Fritz's victories, and convinced of the rightness of the Prussian cause, Alice lived in daily fear for Louis' life, and watched friends and neighbours steadily overwhelmed until enemy troops arrived in Darmstadt itself. It says a great deal for the relationship between the two sisters that they remained close, during and after the war.

'Prince Christian Victor of Schleswig-Holstein, Brevet Major and Captain King's Royal Rifle Corps, September 1899'. As a serving soldier, Christian Victor saw service in India and Ashanti. In 1898 he fought in the battle of Omdurman, afterwards telling a friend, 'I have seen so much of war that I am fully aware of the horrors of it all, and personally I have arrived at the age when the awful carnage which necessarily follows a modern battle leaves a painful impression.' In October 1899 he received orders for South Africa. He fought through the Natal campaign and the war was drawing to an end when he came down with enteric fever. This brought on an attack of malaria, which he had contracted at Ashanti, and he died in hospital at Pretoria on 29 October 1900.

Edward, Prince of Wales, on a route march with the Grenadier Guards in 1914. The Prince was as keen for active service as the establishment was keen to protect him – 'What does it matter if I am killed? I have four brothers'. He was given an appointment behind the lines and was allowed to visit the Front under certain conditions, but he continued to demand permission to fight. The Prince drove himself hard during the war: he served as a staff officer with distinction but never lost the sense of inadequacy that he felt in comparison with fighting troops.

Edward's brother Albert, as a midshipman on HMS *Collingwood*, in the summer of 1914. Prince Albert, the only other member of the King's family old enough for active service, was not protected like his brother. In May 1916, as a sub-lieutenant on *Collingwood*, he took part in the battle of Jutland, but his spells at sea were constantly interrupted by stomach trouble and in 1917 he required an operation for a duodenal ulcer. In 1918 he transferred to the newly formed Royal Air Force.

Kaiser Wilhelm II and his sons Crown Prince Wilhelm (left) and Oskar returning to Vth Army Headquarters after morning service, 23 April 1916. The Kaiser's sons were older men and would all see active service. The Crown Prince commanded the German Vth Army while his brothers served as front line officers, except Prince Adalbert who was in the Navy.

Crown Prince Wilhelm with his fifth child and first daughter Alexandrine, born in April 1915. Her godparent was the entire Vth Army, a gesture that was repeated in September 1917 when Wilhelm's brother Adalbert had a daughter, Viktoria Marina. Her godparent was the Grenadier Regiment 'King Frederick the Great', the 3rd East Prussian Regiment number 4; and a select group of officers and men was photographed standing rather self-consciously round her cradle.

Prince Eitel Freidrich, the Kaiser's second son, with his wife Princess Sophie Charlotte of Oldenburg. Eitel Freidrich commanded the First Regiment of Guards through some of the worst fighting of the war. He had a weight problem all his life, but the large exterior concealed a sensitive and at times lonely man with an intense love of the natural world. 'I find people can disappoint you,' he told a friend, 'but never nature.'

Ernst Ludwig of Hesse, Grand Duchess Eleonore and their sons, Georg Donatus and Ludwig, in the garden of the Neues Palais, Darmstadt, in 1916. For Princess Alice's children in particular the war was hard. Ernst Ludwig had one sister in Germany and three on the other side, in England and in Russia. He was no soldier and commanded his own Hessian troops in name only, visiting the areas where they were posted and doing his utmost for the wounded. From the beginning he foresaw disaster. 'We were in Wolfsgarten when the mobilisation orders came, and we hurried away back to Darmstadt', he wrote. 'It was a terrible time when men were fired by an excitement and enthusiasm one can simply not imagine. Throughout the day and night people sang patriotic songs at the top of their voices. The declaration of war pushed their enthusiasm to fever pitch. From our bedroom (we had all the windows open because of the heat) we could hear them singing all over the Altstadt. It was an indescribable feeling, to hear these young men's voices raised in song in the darkness and to know they were all marching to death. Often it was almost unbearable.'

Ernst Ludwig's sister Alix, Tsaritsa of Russia, in 1915. They kept in intermittent contact during the war through neutral Sweden, or by personal messengers like Miss Eady, the Hesse boys' English nurse. Forced to leave Germany in 1915, she was unable to find work in England and made her way to Russia, where Alix befriended her.

Irene of Hesse, Princess Henry of Prussia, with her husband Prince Henry and sons Waldemar (right) and Sigismund during the war. Prince Henry commanded the German Navy, and Sigismund is photographed here in naval uniform. Waldemar's haemophilia made active service impossible, but he wears the uniform of the German Volunteer Ambulance Corps.

Prince Louis of Battenberg, the British First Sea Lord in 1914 with his sons, George (right) and Louis. By a supreme irony the opposing navies at the start of the war were commanded by brothers-in-law; Prince Louis was married to Irene's elder sister Victoria. But after a few months anti-German feeling among the British public forced him to resign. It was unjust. The Prince had taken British nationality voluntarily at the age of fourteen and those who knew him had no doubt of his loyalty, but there was no way they could let this be known. Prince George of Battenberg continued on active service and the younger Prince Louis (above left) joined him as a midshipman shortly after Jutland. When the same tide of anti-German feeling forced the royal family to abandon German names and titles their family name became 'Mountbatten'.

In 1899, when young Alfred of Saxe-Coburg died, Arthur of Connaught and Charlie of Albany were schoolboys at Eton. Either could have been chosen as heir to his uncle Affie in Saxe-Coburg: as events turned out, it was Charlie. The sharp difference in their fates became obvious in war time. Arthur went into the war as a British officer on General French's staff (above); Charlie (now Karl Eduard) as a German prince commanding his own army (right) – but he was also in England with his mother and sister when hostilities began, and was forced rather hurriedly to resign his colonelcy in the Seaforth Highlanders. The family had made him a German prince and he had to fight for his country – but the British press and public hated him for it. Arthur, meanwhile, had a Prussian mother and first cousins in the Prussian Army – and both men were cousins of the Kaiser, and also of the King.

Even death could not reunite the family in war time. On Sunday, 28 October 1917, Princess Helena's husband died at their London home. He was eighty-six. Under normal circumstances the chief mourner would have been his only surviving son Albert of Schleswig-Holstein but he was in Germany, having made a very reluctant move there nearly thirty years before. So at Prince Christian's funeral on 1 November 1917, the coffin was followed by the British Prince Albert, King George V and the Duke of Connaught, in front, and in the second row, from the left, the Duke of Teck, Prince Henry, and Prince Louis of Battenberg. Helena telegraphed the Lord Mayor, thanking him for his condolences on her husband's death; 'There never was a truer Englishman or one more devoted to England than our beloved Prince.'

George V visiting a munitions factory.

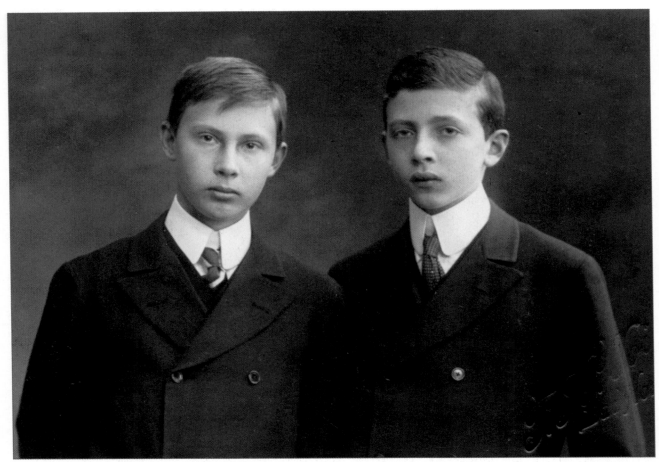

The Queen's family did not escape the casualty lists. The eldest sons of Margarete of Prussia and Friedrich Karl of Hesse-Cassel, Princes Friedrich Wilhelm (left) and Maximilian, were both killed in action; Max in the early months of the war and 'Freddy' in 1916 at Kara Orman in Romania. Both had been brought up to understand that war was not the glamorous, exciting business that propaganda often portrayed in the years before 1914. Their cousin's governess, Miss Topham, recalled an incident in the winter of 1903 when the Kaiser's children stood admiring a military painting until Max commented 'My father says war isn't like that at all. . . . He says it's not so clean and bright and that shells tear the men and horses to pieces and it's horrible. He says no one dares paint war pictures as they really are'. He was just eight years old.

Opposite: Mourning card for Prince Max sold in aid of Hessian troops in Alsace-Lorraine. Max entered the war as a nineteen-year-old subaltern in the Prussian 1st Hussars. In October 1914 his column of cavalry was resting at the monastery on the Mont des Cats, near Bailleul in Belgium. The British 3rd Cavalry Brigade found them and Max was wounded in the fighting: he died in the abbot's care on 13 October. When local people heard that the Kaiser's nephew had been killed they carried the body down to the valley and buried it secretly in the village of Caestre. The priest refused to identify the grave until German troops had left Belgium and full compensation had been paid. In 1920 the grieving parents sent their son Wolfgang to the British authorities to appeal for help. An enquiry was made, and eventually Max's body was returned to his family.

The original caption on the postcard reads: 'The Princes of Battenberg for King and Country. The late Prince Maurice, Lieut. King's Royal Rifle Corps – killed in action 27th Oct. Prince Alexander, 2nd Lieut. Grenadier Guards – invalided home. Prince Leopold, Lieut, King's Royal Rifle Corps – still at the Front.' Alexander (centre) was wounded in the leg at the battle of the Aisne. His brother Leopold, on the right, may have been in France as the card suggests, but his haemophilia made anything but a staff appointment out of the question. The Duke of Connaught had no doubt that Maurice was the strongest of Beatrice's sons and the one the others looked up to, youngest though he was. Maurice was an attractive, high-spirited young man, no different from thousands of other subalterns who went to war in 1914. He was fascinated by flying and fast cars: in May 1914 he was fined £3 for speeding – 34 mph along Hampton Court Road. He fought at Mons in August 1914 and survived the long retreat that followed. He fought on the Aisne, and on 27 October, exactly a week after his cousin Max's death and a few miles to the north, he was leading an attack on a German position in the Ypres salient when a shell burst near him. He died on his way to the dressing station. Prince Arthur of Connaught was serving in the same area and chose a site for the grave, in the town cemetery at Ypres. Arthur represented the family at the funeral, straining to hear the Chaplain's voice over the sound of guns.

Prince Adalbert of Prussia, the Kaiser's third son, and his wife Adelheid of Saxe-Meiningen. They were married at the Naval base at Wilhelmshaven on 3 August 1914, the day Germany declared war on France. The invasion of Belgium had already begun and on the next day, 4 August 1914, Britain would enter the war.

Alexandra of Edinburgh and Saxe-Coburg, Princess Ernst of Hohenlohe-Langenburg with her daughters and future son-in-law in 1915: (l to r) Princess Irma, Alexandra herself, her daughter Alexandra, Duke Friedrich of Schleswig-Holstein-Glücksburg, Princess Marie Melita. Princess Alexandra is wearing nurse's uniform – a sign of the war work which many royal ladies on both sides felt drawn to do as a contribution to the war effort. Friedrich and Marie Melita were married in February 1916.

Another war-time wedding: Prince George of Battenberg and Countess Nadejda Mikhailovna de Torby, the daughter of an exiled Russian Grand Prince, were married in the Chapel of the Russian Embassy in London and at the Chapel Royal, St James's Palace on 15 November 1916.

Queen Mary with her daughter Princess Mary, in the uniform of a VAD (Voluntary Aid Detachment) nurse. Princess Mary was seventeen when war broke out and supported her mother's war work, visiting hospitals and charitable organisations and becoming involved in various projects to assist soldiers and their families. At Christmas 1914 a 'Princess Mary's Gift Box', containing cigarettes or chocolate, was given to every soldier in the British army. In 1918 Mary qualified as a VAD nurse and was posted to Great Ormond Street Hospital.

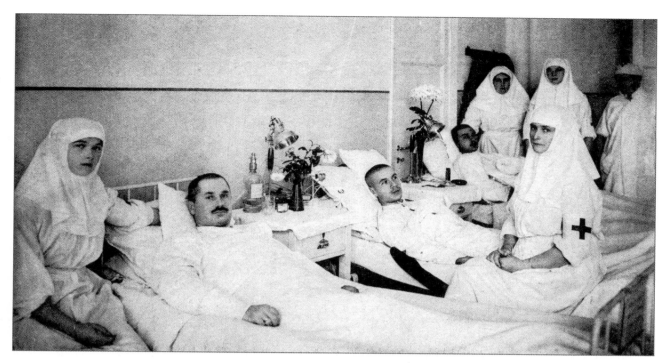

Tsaritsa Alexandra Feodorovna (seated, right) in the Tsarskoe Selo Palace Hospital in 1914 with her daughters Olga (left) and Tatiana (directly behind her mother). An intensely shy woman with very poor health, Alexandra passed through a proper nursing course and encouraged her daughters to do the same, then worked diligently in the hospital she herself had founded, nursing wounded soldiers and assisting with the most distressing operations and dressings. She took individual cases to heart and befriended the men, but her work did not gain universal support. Some criticised her for not taking a more prominent role while others could never forget that she was born in Germany. The nurse next to Tatiana is Alexandra's friend Anna Vyrubova.

Queen Marie of Romania took to nurse's uniform with her characteristic flair, leading from the front and nursing the wounded with her own hands at the same time, working to the point of exhaustion. On 26 August 1917 she wrote in her diary, 'it is an almost sacred pride to me that all our troops want to have me in their midst, more especially when they are to be under fire. I help to keep alive the spirit of enthusiasm. My nurse's dress has become to them a symbol. As I moved all white amongst them, their reflectors singling me out, I knew that I represented the star of hope.'

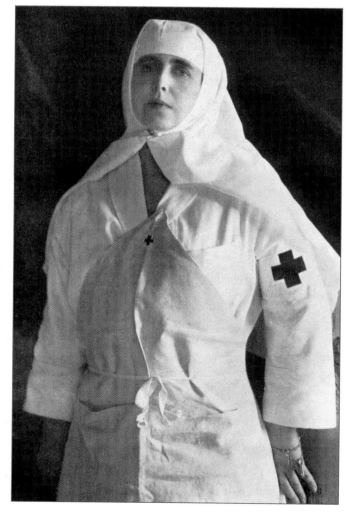

Crown Prince Wilhelm's sons, in white sailor suits: (l to r) Wilhelm, Hubertus and Louis Ferdinand, and their mother Crown Princess Cecilie, surrounded by wounded soldiers. The war effort became something in which even the youngest could play their part.

Prince Ernst August, Duke of Brunswick, eldest child of the Kaiser's daughter Viktoria Luise. He was born in March 1914 and at his christening in May the list of godfathers read like a roll-call of European sovereigns: the Kaiser, Emperor Franz Josef of Austria, the Tsar of Russia, King George V, King Ludwig III of Bavaria, the Grand Duke of Mecklenburg-Schwerin. . . . Within weeks the godfathers had taken their place at the head of the opposing armies and for the first Christmas of the war even the baby was called into service. This was one of a series of photographs of him sold to raise money for the soldiers of Brunswick.

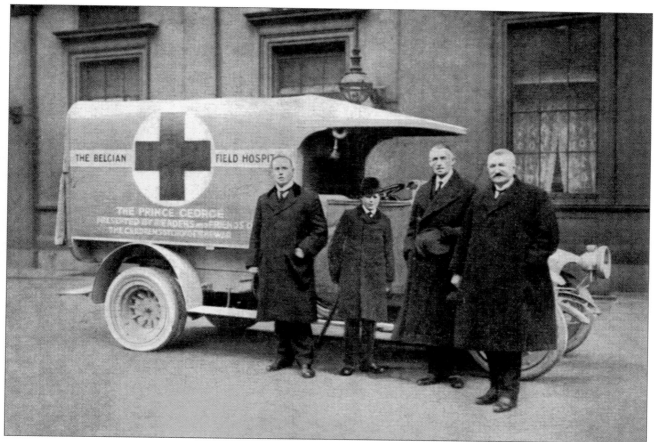

Prince George in the courtyard of Buckingham Palace with Mr Hansell (second right) and representatives of *The Children's Story of the War* and of the Belgian Field Hospital, 26 January 1916. *The Children's Story* was a weekly magazine which sought to explain the campaigns of the war to British children and to find war projects in which they could become involved. Readers were invited to subscribe to a new motor ambulance for the Belgian Field Hospital, and Queen Mary gave permission for her fourteen-year-old son to give his name to the appeal and to be listed as a subscriber. The official handover, shown here, was his first public engagement: readers were told that he 'spent a full half-hour in examining the motor ambulance and the hand ambulance which accompanied it, and was highly pleased with all that he saw.'

Tsesarevich Alexei Nikolaievich of Russia in field uniform. Other royal children performed small engagements or were photographed to raise money for war charities, but Alexei actually went to headquarters with his father and made several tours of the front line. He was fascinated by all he saw and spoke naturally with the men; they in turn were curious to see him and his presence made a deep impression – though concern for his health posed an extra strain on his father.

161

The Greek royal children in 1916: (l to r) George, Paul, Helen, Irene (behind), Katherine, Alexander. The war's effects were felt even in the neutral countries. In Greece the Allies, particularly the French, used the fact that Queen Sophie was the Kaiser's sister to launch a relentless assault of propaganda against her. She was even accused of trying to murder her husband. In 1917 the King was forced to leave the country. The Allies would not accept his eldest son George as King – he had trained with the Prussian Army – and Prince Alexander, the second son, was pushed into the position. The rest of the family was forced to leave Greece and they were allowed no contact with him. Alexander could be no more than a puppet-king. His one independent action was marriage, finding relief from his isolation in a morganatic marriage to a Greek girl, Aspasia Manos. In October 1920 he was bitten on the ankle by a vineyard-keeper's pet monkey while walking his dog: blood-poisoning set in and he died – his mother was not even allowed to return to his bedside.

Opposite: Daisy of Connaught, Crown Princess Margaret of Sweden, with her children Ingrid (right) and Carl Johan, in 1917. Sweden was also neutral but the Queen, by birth a Princess of Baden, and her Court were entirely German in sympathy. This made life very difficult for Daisy who was forced to keep her feelings to herself and work only for Sweden. She created a sewing society to support the Red Cross. When paraffin supplies ran low she organised a candle collection and in November 1917 she instituted a scheme to train girls to work on the land. She also acted as a point of contact for relatives divided by the war. With her help, private letters could be passed on and requests to trace men missing in action. She was also tireless in her work on behalf of prisoners.

The public face of grief; King George V placing a wreath on the coffin of the Unknown Soldier during the procession to Westminster Abbey, on 11 November 1920.

And the private face: Queen Ena of Spain kneeling by the grave of her brother Maurice in Ypres Town Cemetery.

9

The World Between the Wars

The family ties weakened by the death of Queen Victoria and her elder children in the first ten years of the new century were finally severed by the First World War. Fewer and fewer of those still living could even remember the Queen and all had cousins they would now see as foreign. Time brings change to all families, but here the divisions were sharpened by awareness of nationality and the memories of war. Most of Victoria's family in Russia had been murdered by the Bolsheviks. Germany had also been swept by Communist revolution in November 1918; it left dangerous political instability in its wake and no reigning princes. After 1918 many of the Queen's descendants had to come to terms with a world which no longer wanted their services. For those lucky enough to have kept their thrones, in Scandinavia, in the Balkans and southern Europe, and in Britain, royal duties continued, and for them all, reigning and dispossessed, there were births, marriages and deaths, and the normal events of family life.

Prince Joachim of Prussia and his son Karl Franz Josef in 1919–20. As a captain in a front line regiment Joachim had seen active service and been wounded during the war. He was depressed by the collapse of his father's throne and by his own failing marriage to Princess Marie Auguste of Anhalt. So he moved to Lugano in Switzerland where he spent most of his time gambling. In March 1920 Joachim hoped that a coup in Berlin, the 'Kapp Putsch', would overthrow the government and restore the monarchy: when it failed he had no hope left. He shot himself in July. The news was the final blow for his mother – Joachim had always been her favourite – and she died at Doorn in the Netherlands in April 1921, after a long and slow decline.

The Kaiser with his second wife, Princess Hermine Reuss. Wilhelm was forced into exile in the Netherlands at the end of the war and the Kaiserin followed. They settled at Haus Doorn, near Amerongen. The Allies demanded a war crimes trial but the Queen of the Netherlands would not hand Wilhelm over, and once the danger was passed he settled in some state. He was genuinely shaken by the death of his first wife but soon began to look for a replacement. Later he would say that he was reminded of Hermine, who was nearly thirty years his junior, by a letter of sympathy from her young son. Her husband had died a few days before the Kaiserin: he invited her to Doorn in June 1922 and they were married before the year's end.

Prince Oskar of Prussia and his son, also Oskar, in December 1923. When the Kaiser and Crown Prince Wilhelm were forced into exile, the younger sons were able to choose where they lived. Oskar stayed in Berlin, and was tipped by some as a future regent in the event of a restoration, with the Crown Prince's teenage son as Kaiser – a scenario many people were keen to see. Oskar's own marriage was morganatic. A few weeks before the war he secured permission to marry one of his mother's ladies in waiting, Countess Ina-Marie von Bassewitz, much against his father's will. They were happy, and by 1923 had four children – young Oskar was the eldest.

The 'Henrys' of Prussia in their garden at Hemmelmark near Eckernförde in 1927: (l to r) Prince Sigismund, his mother Princess Irene, Prince Henry holding their grandson Alfred (Sigismund's son), Princess Charlotte Agnes (Sigismund's wife), Princess Calixta (Prince Waldemar's wife) and their daughter Barbara; Princess Calixta (Prince Waldemar's wife) and Waldemar himself.

Victoria Melita, Grand Princess Kirill of Russia, with her husband Grand Prince Kirill, son Vladimir and younger daughter Kira at St Briac in Brittany in 1928. Victoria Melita and her family escaped from Russia because Kirill took an oath of allegiance to the Provisional Government before the Tsar's abdication; many members of his own family would never forgive him. But he was next in line to the throne, after the Tsar, the Tsesarevich and Grand Prince Mikhail, the Tsar's brother. As it became obvious that all three were dead, he was persuaded to state his own claim: in 1922 as 'Curator of the Throne' and in 1924 as 'Emperor and Autocrat of all the Russias'. The case is disputed to this day, but on a personal level, the shock of revolution had left Kirill's physical health poor and his mental state fragile. He needed something to fight for and Victoria Melita knew this and encouraged him. They lived in Coburg for a time and both were attracted by the Nazi Party in its early days.

King George II of the Hellenes and his wife Queen Elisabetha in the early 1920s. George was the eldest son of King Constantine I and Queen Sophie, and elder brother of the ill-fated King Alexander. He adored Princess Elisabetha of Romania, Queen Marie's eldest daughter, for nine years and in 1920 she finally agreed to marry him. They were married in 1921, divorced in 1935. George came to the throne on his father's abdication in 1922, went into exile in 1924, returned in 1935, and was forced to leave again when the Germans invaded in 1941, returning at the end of the war. He had no children.

Queen Marie of Yugoslavia (Princess Marie of Romania) with her eldest son Peter in September 1923.

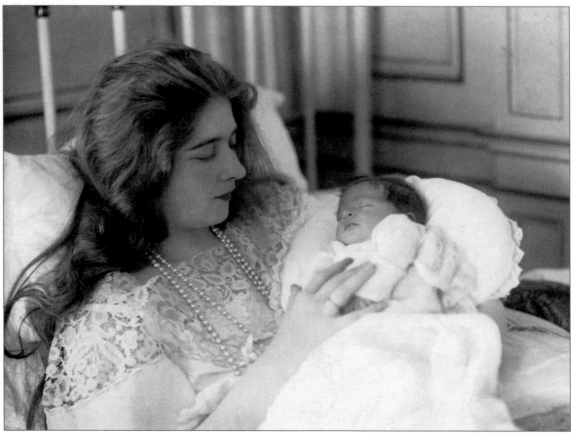

Crown Prince Carol of Romania with his fiancée Princess
Helen of Greece in 1921. Carol was twenty-seven when he
became engaged and already had a chequered past. In 1918
he began an affair with a Romanian girl, Joana Lambrino.
His parents were not unduly concerned until he told them
that he had decided to marry her and renounce his right to
the throne – then, without waiting for a reaction, he
deserted his regiment and married her secretly in Odessa,
behind enemy lines. Carol was brought back and placed in
confinement while the arguments about his future raged.
The war ended. In January 1919 the marriage was annulled
without agreement from Carol – he did not agree until a
year later, when he was already involved with another
woman. His parents sent him on an eight-month tour and
he returned during the celebrations for his sister Elisabetha's
engagement; to everyone's surprise, in October he
announced his intention to marry her fiancé's sister. Helen's
family was dubious – understandably – but she agreed and
they were married on 10 March 1921.

Queen Sophie of the Hellenes with her grandson Prince
Michael of Romania, only child of her daughter Helen and
Crown Prince Carol, in 1922.

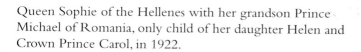

Queen Marie of Romania with her grandsons, King Michael of Romania and Crown Prince Peter of Yugoslavia in January 1928. Michael had inherited the throne six months earlier, when his grandfather King Ferdinand died. The Crown Prince, his father, had refused to return to Romania after Queen Alexandra's funeral in England. Instead, he joined his latest mistress in Paris and renounced his rights to the throne. This time his renunciation was accepted as final. Like Michael, Peter was also to become King while he was still a child.

Prince Nicolas of Romania, in about 1928. Nicolas was Queen Marie's second son. He was at Eton for a time and served in the British Navy, and when his father died he became regent for his nephew Michael. But Nicolas had no interest in politics; in 1930 he willingly involved himself in a plan to bring his brother back to the country – as regent, it was said. Instead, with public backing, Carol managed to establish himself as King Carol II, deposing his son.

Crown Prince Peter of Yugoslavia, *c.* 1927.

Peter with his brothers, Tomislav (left) and Andrej in Zagreb in 1933.

Queen Ena of Spain with her children in the early 1920s: (l to r) Infanta Maria Cristina, Alfonso, Prince of the Asturias, the Queen with her youngest son, Infante Gonzalo, Infante Jaime (behind) and Infante Juan, Infanta Beatriz. Spain was neutral in the war, and the 1920s were Ena's best years. More confident in herself, she had found friends outside the Court and ordinary people were beginning to see the value of her welfare work. But she was still disapproved of at Court and her husband was unfaithful. In the political world too, the situation worsened as the decade drew to an end. In April 1931 the royal family was forced into exile.

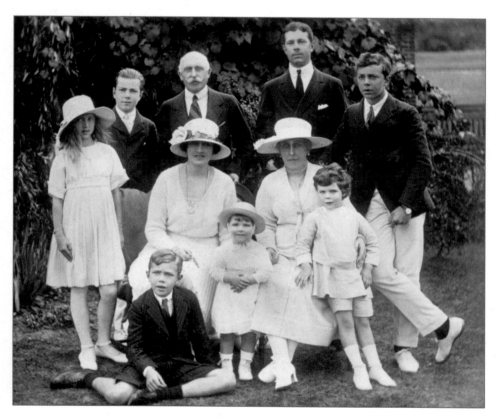

The Duke of Connaught and his family in England in 1921: (l to r) Princess Ingrid of Sweden, her brother Prince Sigvard, the Duke behind his daughter Patsy – Lady Patricia Ramsay – with her nephew Prince Bertil (on the grass) and her son Alexander; Princess Helena Victoria with Prince Carl Johan of Sweden and (behind) Crown Prince Gustav Adolf and his son Prince Gustav Adolf, Duke of Västerbotten. The Crown Princess of Sweden, Daisy, the Duke's elder daughter, had died suddenly in 1920.

In 1923 Crown Prince Gustav Adolf was married again, to Lady Louise Mountbatten (formerly Princess Louise of Battenberg, the younger daughter of Louis of Battenberg and Victoria of Hesse). During the Second World War she kept the lines of communication open for the family just as Crown Princess Margaret, 'Daisy', had done. She reigned as Gustav Adolf's consort in Sweden for twenty-three years.

Prince Arthur of Connaught with his wife Princess Alexandra, Duchess of Fife and their son Alastair Arthur, Earl of Macduff. Alexandra was the elder daughter of Princess Louise of Wales, Duchess of Fife; after her father's death at Aswan in 1912 she was allowed to inherit the Fife dukedom in her own right.

George (left) and Gerald Lascelles, the sons of Princess Mary, George V and Queen Mary's daughter, on the beach at Littlehampton in 1927.

Elizabeth, Duchess of York, holding Princess Elizabeth in 1926. An early glimpse of the future Queen Elizabeth II.

Lady Patricia Ramsay with her son, Master Alexander Ramsay of Mar, *c.* 1927. Lady Patricia, once the darling of the British press, chose to marry one of her father's ADCs, the Hon. Alexander Ramsay. At first her father would not hear of the marriage, but he agreed and the couple enjoyed the first royal wedding to be celebrated in Westminster Abbey since the thirteenth century. Patricia gave up her royal titles but remained a member of the royal family, present on State and family occasions. She was a gifted artist.

At Elsick House, Scotland, in 1931: (l to r in front) Lady Maud Carnegie (younger sister of the Duchess of Fife and a granddaughter of Edward VII), Queen Mary holding Maud's son James, Master of Carnegie, Princess Helena Victoria; (behind) Charles, Lord Carnegie, his father the 10th Earl of Southesk, Miss Bruce, Princess Alice of Athlone (née Albany – Prince Leopold's daughter), Mr Ewan Morgan.

King George V and Queen Mary at Ascot in the early 1930s, riding with their sons Edward, Prince of Wales (in black) and Prince Henry, Duke of Gloucester.

Lady May Cambridge (Princess May of Teck), with her bridesmaid Princess Elizabeth of York. On 24 October 1931 Lady May, Prince Leopold's granddaughter, married Sir Henry Abel Smith at Balcombe in Sussex.

The Duke of Connaught with his granddaughter Ingrid and her husband Frederik, Crown Prince of Denmark, *c.* 1935. Princess Ingrid married Crown Prince Frederik in Stockholm on 24 May 1935 – the 116th anniversary of Queen Victoria's birth. Frederik became King of Denmark in April 1947.

Prince Gustav Adolf of Sweden, Duke of Västerbotten, with Princess Sibylla and their first child, Princess Margaretha, in 1935. By the 1930s many of the dispossessed German princes, including Sibylla's father, Charlie, the Duke of Saxe-Coburg, had regained their standing and much popular sympathy, though no actual powers. Sibylla's wedding to the second-in-line to the throne of Sweden, and her own second cousin, was celebrated in Coburg with all the pomp of a royal wedding – though the Nazi trappings were an uncomfortable reminder of the darkening of the political sky. The couple had three more daughters after Margaretha and, in 1946, a son, who would become the present King Carl XVI Gustav of Sweden.

Princess Caroline Mathilde of Saxe-Coburg, Countess of Castell-Rüdenhausen, with her children Bertram (left), Conradin (right) and Victoria in 1935. Caroline Mathilde, 'Calma', Sibylla's sister, married Count Friedrich of Castell-Rüdenhausen in 1931. They divorced in May 1938; a month later Calma married Captain Max Otto Schnirring. Both men died in the Second World War; Count Friedrich was killed in action in 1940 and Captain Schnirring died in 1944 after a flying accident. By this time Calma had six children, whom she struggled to bring up alone.

Princess Sophie of Greece and Prince Christoph of Hesse-Cassel, 15 December 1930. The family of Prince and Princess Andrew of Greece (Princess Alice of Battenberg) were rescued from Greece by the British Naval cruiser *Calypso* in 1921 when the Prince faced an almost certain death sentence. The elder daughters, Margarita and Theodora, were almost grown women but their sisters Cecilie and Sophie, and baby brother Philip, grew up in exile. Sophie was the youngest and married first, when she was just sixteen. Her husband Christoph was also her second cousin once removed – one of the younger pair of Hesse-Cassel twins.

Princess Margarita of Greece and her fiancé, Prince Gottfried of Hohenlohe-Langenberg in 1931. Like her sister, Margarita also became engaged to a cousin: Gottfried was the son of Princess Alexandra of Edinburgh and Saxe-Coburg, Affie's third daughter. They married at Langenburg in April 1931.

Royal guests leaving the Schlosskirche in Darmstadt after the wedding of Princess Cecilie of Greece and Hereditary Grand Duke Georg Donatus of Hesse-Darmstadt on 2 February 1931: (l to r) the Marchioness of Milford Haven (Victoria of Hesse), her granddaughter Margarita and Prince Gottfried of Hohenlohe (partly obscured), Grand Duke Ernst Ludwig behind his great-nephew, Prince Philip of Greece, Sophie, Princess Christoph of Hesse-Cassel, Prince Ernst of Hohenlohe-Langenburg (Gottfried's father). This wedding provoked an unexpected demonstration of affection for the Hesse family. So many people came out on the streets to watch the family drive to the service that it became impossible for the cars to proceed. While Cecilie and her father Prince Andrew abandoned their car and tried to push through the crowd on foot, the Grand Duke and his sons led a rescue party, forcing an opening and calling to people to let the bride come to church. Fortunately it was all very good-natured and the wedding was able to go ahead as planned.

Grand Duke Ernst Ludwig, Hereditary Grand Duke Georg Donatus and baby Prince Ludwig Ernst Andreas in 1932. Ernst Ludwig inherited the Hesse throne as a young man with good intentions and ideas but an unstable personality. He craved constant entertainment and activity yet suffered periods of depression, haunted by a succession of family tragedies. His first marriage began well but ended unhappily and it was not until his second marriage that he really seemed to find himself and grow. He faced the November revolution of 1918 with great courage, taking his sons to safety but insisting on returning to the palace himself; the immediate aftermath of the war was a depressing time for him, but by the 1930s he had weathered the storms and found himself respected and valued in Hesse, with a real role still to play. He also had a wife and sons he adored, and grandchildren too – Ludwig, seen here, was the first.

Princess Cecilie of Greece, Hereditary Grand Duchess of Hesse and Georg Donatus's wife, with their second child Alexander in 1933.

Princes Moritz (right) and Heinrich of Hesse-Cassel in 1933. Moritz and Heinrich were the elder sons of Prince Philipp of Hesse-Cassel, one of the first pair of Hesse-Cassel twins. Both boys were born in Italy; their mother was Princess Mafalda, the second daughter of King Victor Emmanuel III, and the young family's time was divided between the two countries.

Princess Theodora of Greece and Prince Berthold of Baden with their children Margarita, Maximilian and baby Ludwig at Schloss Salem in 1937. Theodora was the last of the four Hesse sisters to marry, at Baden-Baden in August 1931.

Ernst Ludwig's grandsons, Ludwig (right) and Alexander, playing in the garden in 1937.

Their mother, Hereditary Grand Duchess Cecilie and baby sister Johanna.

Their uncle, Prince Ludwig, and his fiancée, the Hon. Margaret Geddes at Wolfsgarten, in the summer of 1937. Prince Ludwig was Cultural Attaché at the German Embassy in London in the late 1930s. He met Margaret Geddes at the Winter Olympics at Garmisch in 1936. In the autumn of 1937 they visited Darmstadt together; Ernst Ludwig's health was failing and he died peacefully on 9 October. Ludwig and Margaret's wedding, in London, had to be postponed from 23 October to 20 November, then, on 16 November, his entire family was killed in the plane crash off Ostende (see p. 141). Only fourteen-month-old Johanna escaped – she was not on the plane but was staying with her Baden cousins at Schloss Salem.

Princess Viktoria Luise, the Kaiser's only daughter, with her husband Ernst August, Duke of Brunswick and their children (l to r) Friederike, Ernst August, Welf Heinrich, Georg Wilhelm and Christian, c. 1935. The marriage of the Duke and Duchess of Brunswick would never have happened if it had not been for a car crash. Ernst August's grandfather was Queen Victoria's cousin the King of Hanover. He had lost his kingdom to Prussia after the Austro-Prussian war of 1866: his son, the Duke of Cumberland, Ernst August's father, was notorious for his hatred of the Prussians. But in 1912 the Duke's eldest son was killed in a car crash in Silesia and the Kaiser sent his own sons to mount guard over the body and supervise the escort home. The Duke felt compelled to send his next son to Berlin in gratitude and so the young couple met. The wedding, in 1913, was the last great gathering of European royalty, bringing together the Tsar, the Kaiser and Kaiserin, King George V and Queen Mary and a host of other princes. Nothing quite like it would ever be seen again.

The Crown Prince of Prussia's children in the late 1930s: (l to r) Friedrich, Cecilie, Wilhelm, Alexandrine and Louis Ferdinand. Crown Princess Cecilie insisted on remaining in Germany at the end of the war with her children when their father and grandfather were forced into exile. There was talk of a restoration, with young Wilhelm as Kaiser. Once the political situation had stabilised Cecilie placed her elder sons in a school in Potsdam, moving to Silesia herself with the younger children because the cost of living was cheaper. In 1925 the elder princes were taken on a tour of Prussia – officially private, visiting friends, but with a number of semi-official engagements. But their position was still sensitive. In 1926 young Wilhelm's appearance in uniform on military exercises provoked such anger that the Chief of the Army Command was forced to resign. Louis Ferdinand was the family rebel – in America in 1929 he had a celebrated affair with an actress, Lily Damita; his family acted swiftly to move him out of danger. The Crown Prince and Princess hoped to find a royal bride for Wilhelm but in 1933 he proposed to Dorothea von Salviati, whom he met as a student at Bonn. To marry her he had to surrender his right to the throne. Then, much to their parents' delight, in 1937 Louis Ferdinand found a bride who could not have been more acceptable, Kira Kirillovna of Russia, the younger daughter of Victoria Melita and Grand Prince Kirill.

Kira Kirillovna of Russia with the Kaiser's second wife Hermine, at Doorn in 1937. Curiously, pride of place is given to the photo of the dead Kaiserin Auguste Viktoria in the centre of the table, towards which the eyes of her successor are turned. The photo beside it shows the Kaiser himself, the other looks like one of Hermine's sons by her first marriage. Kira and Louis Ferdinand were married twice: the civil and Orthodox ceremonies were held at Schloss Cecilienhof, the Crown Prince's Potsdam home, on 2 May 1937. Then the whole company adjourned to Doorn in the Netherlands for a Lutheran service in the presence of the Kaiser. Both weddings were held in considerable state, with all the uniforms, decorations and finery of the old world.

The Kaiser with the bride after the wedding service at Doorn.

Maria Kirillovna, Princess Karl of Leiningen, with her children Emich, Karl, Kira and Margarita in 1935. Maria was Victoria Melita and Kirill's elder daughter. In November 1925 she married Prince Karl of Leiningen, a descendant of Queen Victoria's half-brother. He was to die in a Russian prisoner-of-war camp in 1946 – a fate shared by a number of German princes.

Queen Maud of Norway with her granddaughters, Ragnhild (left) and Astrid, in 1937. Maud's only child, Crown Prince Olav, married Princess Märtha of Sweden in March 1929: Ragnhild, always the smaller of their daughters, was actually the elder. Queen Maud spent much of her time in later years in England. By 1936 she was the last surviving child of Edward VII and Queen Alexandra and she remained a close and supportive friend to her widowed sister-in-law Queen Mary. She made her last public appearance in England at the 1937 Coronation. In October 1938 she was taken ill while on a shopping trip to London; after several weeks in a nursing home she had an operation but died soon after.

Princess Elizabeth (right) and Princess Margaret Rose at the last of the Duke of York's Camps, at Balmoral in August 1939. In 1919 the Princesses' father, then Duke of York, had become President of the Boys' Welfare Association – a position he would accept only on condition that no ceremonial would be attached. He wanted to draw closer to ordinary people and devoted time and consideration to the project for the next twenty years, visiting factories and institutions and organising annual camps for boys in their late teens – half from industrial backgrounds and half from the public schools. The camps were held in the grounds of Balmoral and he and his family acted as hosts and joined in with many of the activities.

Right: Prince George, Duke of Kent and Princess Marina with Prince Edward and Princess Alexandra, in 1940. George was the most academic of George V's sons and the most interested in the arts: an education at Eton like his brother Henry's might have suited him, but instead he was sent to the Naval College at Osborne. He proved to be a bad sailor; after a rather rootless period working as a civil servant by day and tasting London society by night he became engaged to Princess Marina of Greece in August 1934. They were married in November. The Duke began the Second World War in Naval Intelligence before transferring to the RAF. In July 1942 his second son, Michael, was born. A friend wrote in her diary, 'The Duke seems to love this tiny infant. Every evening, instead of sitting late as usual, he leaves the table shortly after ten o'clock and carries his youngest son to the nursery and lays him in his cot and stands watching and watching. Nannie told me that each night as he lays his son in his cot, she discreetly leaves the room but she can hear the Duke talking softly to him. Perhaps he is unconsciously preparing him for the future.' The Duke was killed in a plane crash in August 1942 on his way to Iceland.

10

And Finally . . .

By the end of 1940 a hundred years had passed since the birth of Queen Victoria's first child. In that time there had been over 240 descendants of the Queen and 180 of them were still living, spanning four generations. Besides being royal, which they could not help, the family had produced writers, artists, sportsmen, musicians, and men and women who are still remembered for their commitment to nursing and other fields of welfare work. Like any other family they had faced personal difficulties and issues of national and international importance: by 1940 Europe was once again at war.

And finally, by 1940, a new generation of future monarchs was making its appearance . . .

Kaiser Wilhelm II with his great-grandson Friedrich Wilhelm in 1939. Queen Victoria's first grandchild remains one of the most controversial of her descendants. His parents hoped to produce a progressive liberal prince in the British constitutional tradition; they watched him become a reactionary Prussian nationalist, opposed to everything they stood for. Yet always with Wilhelm there are contradictions. He despised and envied England but also loved the country and felt that he belonged. He never forgot how the old Queen had died resting on his good arm – for two-and-a-half hours he had supported her pillow, unable to change his position. He inherited and developed the most militaristic of regimes, yet shrank from actual war. Wilhelm was pushed to the sidelines as the First World War progressed because his generals, and even his wife and eldest son, believed that he would not be sufficiently aggressive against Britain. In public and in private his statements were violently anti-Semitic, yet the persecution of the Jews in the late 1930s made him say he was ashamed to be German. He could be overbearing and loud with a cruel sense of humour, but he was also capable of sensitivity and kindness. Wilhelm's last years were spent peacefully at Doorn, sawing wood and writing his memoirs. The British government offered him refuge in England in 1940 but he refused: he also refused an invitation to return to Germany. He died in 1941 and was buried – at his own request and much to Hitler's annoyance – at Doorn, with no Nazi insignia.

Once considered very daring, Crown Prince Wilhelm and Crown Princess Cecilie were the 'bright young things' of Berlin in the years before the First World War. Both defied convention, but while Cecilie grew into the traditional role of a royal lady, Wilhelm seemed to become more conceited and less willing to perform duties that bored him. Their relationship was passionate and sometimes stormy: Wilhelm's friends believed that Cecilie was jealous of their influence and perhaps they were right. The First World War enforced a separation between husband and wife, and Wilhelm's affairs became notorious – but he and Cecilie also had two more children during the war years. Then came the long separation of his five-year exile, when Cecilie came into her own as active head of their family. Once reunited they continued to work together for their children, though Wilhelm also continued in his womanising. Cecilie too had her moments. Their marriage had become a good working partnership in which each knew the strengths and weaknesses of the other. Wilhelm understood; 'I can only thank my wife from the bottom of my heart for having been to me the best and most faithful friend and companion . . . full of comprehension for what I am, holding to me unswervingly in fortune and distress.'

The abdication crisis was the deepest shock the British monarchy faced in the twentieth century. As Prince of Wales, Edward was a great favourite with the public. His post-war tours of the Commonwealth and visits to the United States were immensely successful and helped to enhance the image of the monarchy: like his grandfather Edward VII he had a gift for easy communication which his parents lacked. He was moved by the sufferings he witnessed on his travels and he did want to help, but he lacked the concentration to see anything through to the end or the patience to take advice. At heart he pitied himself, as his published letters show only too clearly. He tried to treat his position as a job which he could break away from when it suited him, to do whatever he wanted to do without criticism – something no prince has ever achieved. Yet in one thing Edward did show absolute determination: in the love he felt for Mrs Simpson, which he refused to set aside no matter what the cost.

Another of the 'problem children' of Queen Victoria's family, King Carol II of Romania emerged from a difficult upbringing as a young man who respected nothing so much his own will. His affairs became notorious, but he was also a highly intelligent man who cared for his country and could have made a very successful monarch – if only things had been different. Seen here with his son Michael in the 1930s, he reigned from 1930 to 1940 and helped to pull the country out of crisis, restoring prosperity and establishing military, cultural and educational institutions. He resisted Hitler, insisting on Romanian neutrality until, in 1940, he was forced into exile and his son once again became King. Carol had his strengths, but to his family, and particularly to his wife Princess Helen and to his mother, he was cruel. In his second exile, after 1940, he married his mistress Elena Lupescu, and he died in Portugal in 1953.

The eldest son of the Crown Prince and Princess, Prince Wilhelm of Prussia was brought up with the idea that he would become Kaiser – an idea that persisted long after the collapse of his grandfather's throne. On marriage he renounced these rights, though his father intended to re-instate him if ever the chance arose. 'He has become a fine person,' the Crown Prince said of his son in 1925, 'quiet, understanding, unusually sober in his thinking, at the same time full of humour.' But the chance did not arise – though many who silently opposed Hitler, particularly in the army, never ceased to hope. Young Wilhelm settled happily with his wife and two small daughters, managing the family estate in the Mark Brandenburg. In the late summer of 1939 he was called up and sent to the 1st Infantry regiment at Köningsberg. He took part in the invasion of Poland and achieved quick promotion. On 23 May 1940 he was leading his company against a French position at Valenciennes when he was wounded, suffering severe internal injuries. He died in a field hospital at Nivelles three days later. His funeral at the Antike Temple in Potsdam was allowed only a brief notice in the newspapers; the Nazis were stunned to see a crowd of at least fifty thousand turn out on the streets. This display of the lasting power of royalty was too much for Hitler. Previously he had accepted the support of the German princes, pleased to use their names and titles where it suited, but his attitude was already hardening. After Wilhelm's funeral he began to move against them.

Opposite: The question of involvement with the Nazi Party is one of the saddest chapters in the long story of the Queen's family. All Germans faced the choice, but the princes were still prominent figures whose decisions would be noticed. Some simply went along with the movement because it had captured the popular will. Some were cautious. Some held back altogether. A few were completely seduced by the promise of a revival in German pride and German fortunes, after the long misery of the post-war years. None was more convinced than August Wilhelm, the Kaiser's fourth son. From childhood 'Auwi' had been the actor in the family and he responded with enthusiasm to the parades, the torchlit rallies, and the carefully orchestrated events that were so important to the public face of Nazism. His sister, Viktoria Luise, said that he disagreed with the Party's racial policies, but this did not stop him becoming a keen Party member. When the Nazis turned against the German princes he was expelled from the Party and arrested; then, at the end of the war, he was interned and tried by the Allies.

Charles Edward, 'Charlie', Duke of Saxe-Coburg, with his family in about 1930; from the left in front, Caroline Mathilde, Charles Edward, Victoria Adelheid, Friedrich Josias; (behind) Johann Leopold, Sibylla, Hubertus. Charles Edward's divided loyalties had made the front line the most comfortable place for him to be during the First World War: the fighting men on both sides shared the same daily experience while the real gulf in understanding lay between the trenches and the home front. He emerged from the war with no reigning powers, but enough land to make him one of the wealthiest men in Germany. Still he was ill-at-ease and gravitated naturally towards the old soldiers' organisation, the Stahlhelm, which proved a magnet for many dispossessed princes. Here Charles Edward first encountered Nazism, and he was won over by the promise of a revived Germany. He attended rallies and in 1933 became President of the German Red Cross. In 1935 he joined the Nazi Party. His one real hope was for better relations with Britain and he dedicated himself to this through active presidency of the Anglo-German Fellowship. He never understood how much had changed since his time at Eton, and how foreign he seemed to his former contemporaries.

Prince Philipp of Hesse-Cassel was studying architecture in Rome in the early 1920s when he first met King Victor Emmanuel's daughter Mafalda. By 1923 they both wished to marry, though Mafalda's family were hoping for an engagement to Prince Leopold, the heir to the Belgian throne. Mafalda had to wait two years before they would give consent: then her grandmother would not hear of a Protestant wedding service. When the couple married at Racconigi in September 1925, Philipp's family stayed away in protest. This was a true love-match, and Philipp and Mafalda divided their time between Germany and Italy. But his standing as son-in-law to the King of Italy attracted the attention of the Nazi Party and they courted his support: he would prove useful as a channel of communication with Fascist Italy. He listened, won over like his cousins by the promise of a new Germany. In 1933 he was appointed Oberpräsident of Hesse-Nassau – an administrative appointment, working with the Nazi Gauleiter in the region whom he came to detest. Once he threatened to resign, but was told that his enemy would simply be given his place. Philipp was a gentle, shy man whose consuming interest was his art collection. Privately he used his position and his money to secure passports for Jews and help them escape to the Netherlands. Publicly he continued his official duties, occasionally taking personal missions to Italy for Hitler. His fortunes changed in 1943. That spring he was summoned to Headquarters, ostensibly to work but more particularly as a potential hostage: in September, after the capitulation of Italy, he was arrested and imprisoned. Mafalda was tricked into Nazi hands in Rome and flown to Berlin, then interned in Buchenwald concentration camp under the name of 'Frau Weber'. She was injured during an American bombing raid in August 1944 and died soon afterwards. Her family did not find out until the following spring.

Princess Mafalda with her sons Moritz (left) and Heinrich, *c.* 1933. After the capitulation of Italy, Philipp and Mafalda's children, Moritz, Heinrich, Otto and Elisabeth, were sent for safety to the Vatican by their Italian grandmother Queen Elena. There they stayed, until Prince Philipp's family arranged to move them to Hesse. The rest of their war was spent sheltering with relatives at Kronberg or with Prince Ludwig and Princess Margaret of Hesse-Darmstadt in Wolfsgarten.

Alice, Princess Andrew of Greece, *c.* 1916. Princess Andrew returned to Greece in 1935 with plans to devote herself to charitable work and ultimately to found an order of nuns. She refused to leave before the approaching German Army. Under the Nazi occupation she continued as before – they took little notice of a princess in a nun's habit caring for orphaned children, never realising that she was also sheltering a Jewish family under the same roof. When questioned she was able to use her deafness as a shield – the Gestapo simply thought her eccentric and never discovered her secret. So the Cohen family were safe until the war ended and Princess Alice went on working in Athens, living in very poor conditions, until forced to leave in the late 1940s. In 1993 she was honoured in the Garden of the Righteous at Yad Vashem in Jerusalem.

Princess Alice is not the only descendant of Queen Victoria considered 'Righteous among the nations'. Princess Helen of Romania was recalled to the country in 1940 when her son Michael became King for a second time. The country was in the grip of a pro-German dictatorship and the persecution of the Jews was brutal. The King and his mother had no actual power but Helen did her utmost to halt the deportations and the violence, appealing to every authority within her reach and putting her own opposition to anti-Semitism on record. She used her devout Orthodoxy to great effect, forming alliance with Orthodox and Catholic Church leaders and in the process saving many thousands of lives. In 1993 she too was honoured at Yad Vashem

Few families can claim a canonised saint among their number. Queen Victoria's can claim seven, their number dramatically increased by the canonisation in August 2000 of the Russian imperial family. That decision was not without its critics and the Orthodox Church authorities were careful to stress that the family had been honoured only for its manner of dying. No such controversy surrounded the canonisation of the Tsaritsa's sister seven years earlier. Grand Princess Elizaveta Feodorovna, 'Ella' of Hesse, was married for over twenty years to Grand Prince Sergei Alexandrovich of Russia, a reserved, unpopular man whom she loved very deeply. His assassination in February 1905 made her withdraw from society to devote her time and resources to charitable work. Profound religious faith was something she and her husband had shared, and in time she decided to found the Martha and Mary Convent of Mercy, an order of nursing nuns, to work in Moscow's poorest districts. She took the veil herself in 1910 and was raised to the rank of abbess, adopting an ascetic way of life with complete sincerity. But she was still the last Tsar's aunt and his wife's sister. Around Easter 1918 she was arrested with one of her nuns and taken east to Ekaterinburg where they joined a larger group of Romanov prisoners deported from Petrograd. In June they were all imprisoned in the schoolhouse at Alapaevsk, and on the night of 17/18 July all eight prisoners were pushed down a mineshaft in the nearby forest. Grenades were thrown in after them and the shaft covered: the bodies were found by investigators of the White Army and taken to China. In 1920 Ella's family arranged for her body and the body of Sister Varvara to be buried in the Orthodox Church of St Mary Magdalene in Jerusalem.

Princess Alice's daughters were strong, interesting women, none more so than the eldest, Victoria, seen here in 1932 with her great-grandson, Ludwig Ernst Andreas of Hesse. She saw her family through a series of tragedies which started when she was still a child, never losing her positive outlook and interest in life. 'I should have been the man of the family', was her own opinion, and Meriel Buchanan, who knew the Hesse family well, added; 'it is true that her lack of personal vanity, her firm handshake, her direct, sometimes rather abrupt, manner, gave an almost masculine impression. She was, however, a woman whose absolute integrity seemed to shine out of her bright blue eyes, whose clear-reasoning brain was remarkable, whose honesty and singleness of purpose made one feel that one could never tell her a lie or indulge in subterfuge or evasion, a woman who had faced the many sorrows life brought her with unflinching courage, for whom it was possible to feel nothing but respect and admiration.'

The third of Princess Alice's 'three graces', Irene was a shy, gentle person; the family peacemaker from childhood onwards. Her brother described her as a busy child, always trying to see the positive side and so anxious to do the right thing and to make sure that the other children did so too that they called her 'Aunt Fuss'. 'In earlier years', he remembered, 'she rode with a light touch and loved to dance, as I did. Often we danced together in empty ballrooms, accompanied by our own singing.' Her married life was not always easy: her husband's temper could be unpredictable and she suffered the anxiety of caring for two haemophilic sons. 'Now her husband is dead after two years of grave illness,' Ernst Ludwig wrote in the 1930s. 'She is alone now, but in spite of this she manages to do so much that she is sometimes completely worn out. Her only thought and concern is to find ways in which she can help people, time and time again.'

Margaret, Princess Ludwig of Hesse-Darmstadt, with her adopted daughter Johanna in 1939. The Hesse family's tradition of remarkable women continued to the end. Margaret began her life in Darmstadt in the worst possible circumstances. Her husband's entire family, save for one baby, was killed in a plane crash on the way to her wedding and her life in the country began with their funeral. She and Ludwig adopted the baby, Johanna, and loved her as their own; Margaret communicated easily with children and looked forward to having a family. She never did, and in June 1939 Johanna died of meningitis. Within months Margaret's own country and her husband's country were at war. Few people could have come through all this so well as she did. By the end of the war she and her husband were providing shelter at Wolfsgarten to a host of dispossessed relatives and friends – and she made sure that they all had a job to do. Margaret was not one to give in to troubles, and in the aftermath of war she and her husband worked tirelessly to help the wounded, orphaned and disabled children and others, and to help in the rehabilitation of Darmstadt. Ludwig died in 1968 and Margaret lived on in Darmstadt, continuing the work they had shared. She was loved and respected by local people, who saw her as one of their own. She died suddenly in 1997 leaving the Landgraf Moritz of Hesse, Prince Philipp and Princess Mafalda's eldest son, as her heir: with her the House of Hesse-Darmstadt had come to an end.

Some princesses played a less helpful part. Princess Beatrice of Saxe–Coburg and Edinburgh, the youngest of Affie's four daughters, had a difficult path to marriage. After an abortive romance with the Tsar's brother Grand Prince Mikhail, doomed to failure because they were first cousins, she met the Infante Alfonso, a cousin of the King of Spain, at the King's wedding in 1906. She liked him, but not the idea of converting to Catholicism. In private the King assured his cousin that he had no objections to the marriage and urged him to go ahead, in Coburg, writing himself to the local Bishop for the necessary dispensation. The couple married, but the Spanish government was not so willing to compromise. The King was compelled to take away his cousin's army commission and royal titles, and the couple set up homes in Coburg and Switzerland, not returning to Spain until 1912. Then Beatrice made mischief in Spain and aggravated the tensions between King Alfonso and Queen Ena, flirting with the King and stirring the Court's antipathy to her cousin the Queen. It is even said that she procured mistresses for the King: his mother certainly believed this and, on her instigation, Beatrice was ordered to leave the country. This photograph was taken around 1924 and shows her with her husband and sons, from the left, Alonso, Ataulfo and Alvaro, who were educated in England. Later she was allowed to return to Spain: when the royal family was forced to leave the country in 1931 Beatrice bravely insisted on staying to look after the King's elderly aunt. Her middle son, Alonso, was killed in action in the Spanish Civil War.

Queen Marie of Romania's youngest daughter, Ileana, was steered into marriage with Archduke Anton of Austria-Tuscany by her brother King Carol after a previous engagement had fallen through. But much to her disappointment, her brother would not allow her to live in Romania so she and her husband settled in Austria: the photo shows her in 1935 with her children Archduke Stefan and Archduchesses Maria Ileana and Alexandra. Anton served in the Luftwaffe in the Second World War and Ileana returned to Romania and founded a hospital at Bran; this, and her children, became her chief objects in life. She was devoted to Romania, but her tendency to act independently and her dabblings in politics caused problems for her nephew Michael. In later life she became an Orthodox nun and helped to establish a monastery in America.

Ileana's sister Elisabetha, who divorced her husband George II of the Hellenes in 1935 and resumed her old title of Princess of Romania. Returning to the country during her brother's reign, she became a constant thorn in the side of her nephew Michael, collaborating with his Communist opponents against him. Elisabetha was a difficult, selfish woman who liked to shock. 'I've committed every vice but one', she is supposed to have said, 'and I don't want to die till I've murdered.'

The younger son of Prince Louis of Battenberg and Princess Victoria of Hesse-Darmstadt, Lord Louis Mountbatten ultimately rose to the rank of First Sea Lord – a vindication of his father who had been forced to resign the same office in 1914 for having a German name, an injustice Lord Louis never forgot. Lord Mountbatten's list of achievements and official appointments are well known: he was equally proud of a sporting achievement made under an assumed name. In the early 1920s he encountered the game of polo in India and he took to it, becoming a top-class player and encouraging the younger men of the royal family to take part. He wrote a book, *An Introduction to Polo*, under the pen-name 'Marco', which has remained the definitive work on the sport.

The royal family has a long tradition of yacht racing and it was in this field that Crown Prince Olav of Norway made his name as a sportsman, winning a gold medal for yachting at the 1928 Olympics.

Prince Albert, Duke of York, the future King George VI, was a keen tennis player in the 1920s; in July 1920 with his partner Louis Greig he won the RAF doubles competition. But their entry into the Wimbledon Championships in 1926 proved unhappy for the Duke. The Club had placed the match on Court Number Two – it would have been the Centre Court if the Duke had not protested – and the size and proximity of the crowd was too much for his nerves; his match was lost in straight sets.

Left: A number of Queen Victoria's descendants have written memoirs – the Kaiser, Princess Marie Louise of Schleswig-Holstein, Princess Victoria of Prussia, Queen Marie of Romania, Princess Ileana, Princess Viktoria Luise, Grand Duke Ernst Ludwig, King Peter and Queen Alexandra of Yugoslavia, Prince Heinrich of Hesse: the list goes on. Princess Alice, Countess of Athlone's *For My Grandchildren*, first published in 1966, is one of the best-loved of these books in English, giving an inside view of the Queen and her family, and their lives in the decades that followed her death. Princess Alice was also the longest-lived of the Queen's descendants, reaching an age of 97 years, 10 months and 9 days at the time of her death in 1981.

Below: By 1940 a new generation of future monarchs was in the wings. Queen Ena's grandson the Infante Juan Carlos of Spain (bottom left, looking out of the picture) inherited a restored throne of Spain in 1975 as King Juan Carlos, one of the most admired of modern sovereigns. He appears here with his grandfather and his sisters and cousins in April 1939: from the left, Don Alfonso (son of Infante Jaime), Infante Juan Carlos (son of Infante Juan), Donna Sandra Torlonia, Don Marco Torlonia (children of the Infanta Beatriz), Infanta Maria del Pilar and Infanta Margarita (daughters of Infante Juan), King Alfonso XIII, Don Gonzalo (son of Infante Jaime).

Queen Frederika of the Hellenes holding her son Constantine, later King Constantine II of the Hellenes, at the time of his christening, in the summer of 1940.

Princess Margrethe of Denmark in 1940. The Princess would succeed her father, Frederik IX, as Queen Margrethe II in 1972.

The third and youngest child of Crown Prince Olav and Crown Princess Märtha, Prince Harald came to the Norwegian throne in 1991 as King Harald V.

Family Trees

It would be hard to imagine a single family tree large enough for all of Queen Victoria's family up to 1940, so

Tree 1 shows the descendants of the Queen's four sons . . .
Tree 2 shows the families of her younger daughters . . .
and for the family of her eldest child,
Victoria, Princess Royal, Crown Princess of Prussia and Empress of Germany,
see Tree 3.

Children born after 1940 are not shown.
Weddings after 1940 are mentioned only if both partners already appear somewhere on the family trees.

Nicknames mentioned in the text also appear on the family trees.

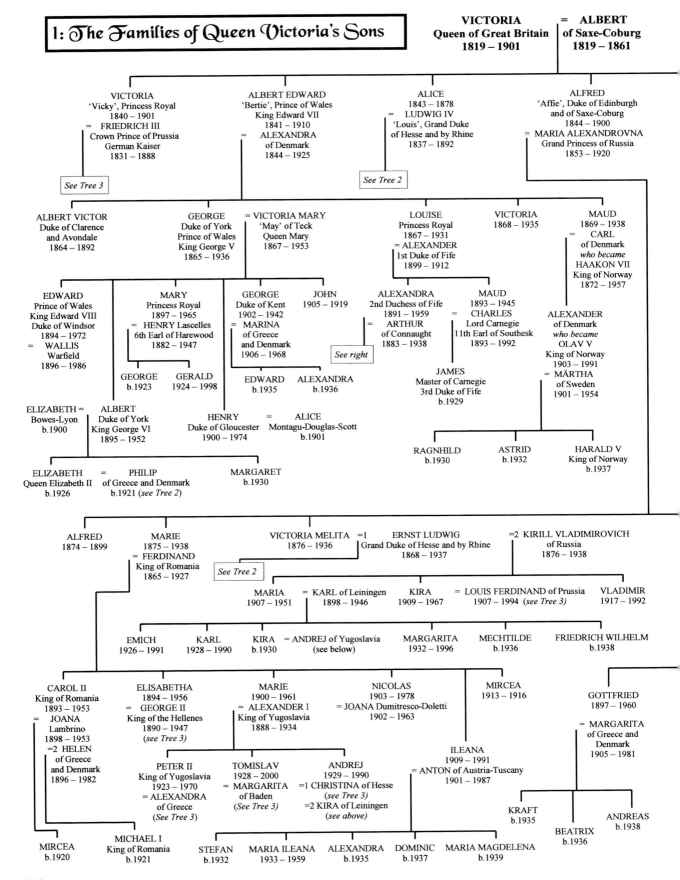

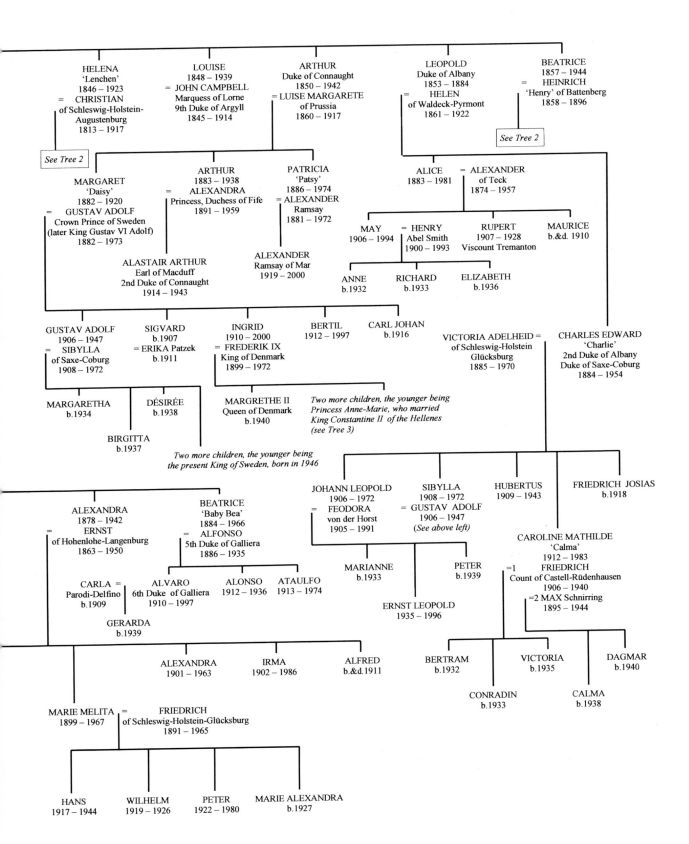

HELENA
'Lenchen'
1846 – 1923
=
CHRISTIAN
of Schleswig-Holstein-
Augustenburg
1813 – 1917

LOUISE
1848 – 1939
= JOHN CAMPBELL
Marquess of Lorne
9th Duke of Argyll
1845 – 1914

ARTHUR
Duke of Connaught
1850 – 1942
= LUISE MARGARETE
of Prussia
1860 – 1917

LEOPOLD
Duke of Albany
1853 – 1884
=
HELEN
of Waldeck-Pyrmont
1861 – 1922

BEATRICE
1857 – 1944
=
HEINRICH
'Henry' of Battenberg
1858 – 1896

See Tree 2

See Tree 2

MARGARET
'Daisy'
1882 – 1920
=
GUSTAV ADOLF
Crown Prince of Sweden
(later King Gustav VI Adolf)
1882 – 1973

ARTHUR
1883 – 1938
=
ALEXANDRA
Princess, Duchess of Fife
1891 – 1959

PATRICIA
'Patsy'
1886 – 1974
= ALEXANDER
Ramsay
1881 – 1972

ALICE
1883 – 1981
= ALEXANDER
of Teck
1874 – 1957

MAY
1906 – 1994
= HENRY
Abel Smith
1900 – 1993

RUPERT
1907 – 1928
Viscount Tremanton

MAURICE
b.&d. 1910

ALASTAIR ARTHUR
Earl of Macduff
2nd Duke of Connaught
1914 – 1943

ALEXANDER
Ramsay of Mar
1919 – 2000

ANNE
b.1932

RICHARD
b.1933

ELIZABETH
b.1936

GUSTAV ADOLF
1906 – 1947
=
SIBYLLA
of Saxe-Coburg
1908 – 1972

SIGVARD
b.1907
= ERIKA Patzek
b.1911

INGRID
1910 – 2000
= FREDERIK IX
King of Denmark
1899 – 1972

BERTIL
1912 – 1997

CARL JOHAN
b.1916

VICTORIA ADELHEID =
of Schleswig-Holstein
Glücksburg
1885 – 1970

CHARLES EDWARD
'Charlie'
2nd Duke of Albany
Duke of Saxe-Coburg
1884 – 1954

MARGARETHA
b.1934

DÉSIRÉE
b.1938

MARGRETHE II
Queen of Denmark
b.1940

*Two more children, the younger being
Princess Anne-Marie, who married
King Constantine II of the Hellenes
(see Tree 3)*

BIRGITTA
b.1937

*Two more children, the younger being
the present King of Sweden, born in 1946*

JOHANN LEOPOLD
1906 – 1972
=
FEODORA
von der Horst
1905 – 1991

SIBYLLA
1908 – 1972
= GUSTAV ADOLF
1906 – 1947
(See above left)

HUBERTUS
1909 – 1943

FRIEDRICH JOSIAS
b.1918

ALEXANDRA
1878 – 1942
=
ERNST
of Hohenlohe-Langenburg
1863 – 1950

BEATRICE
'Baby Bea'
1884 – 1966
=
ALFONSO
5th Duke of Galliera
1886 – 1935

CAROLINE MATHILDE
'Calma'
1912 – 1983
=1
FRIEDRICH
Count of Castell-Rüdenhausen
1906 – 1940
=2 MAX Schnirring
1895 – 1944

CARLA =
Parodi-Delfino
b.1909

ALVARO
6th Duke of Galliera
1910 – 1997

ALONSO
1912 – 1936

ATAULFO
1913 – 1974

MARIANNE
b.1933

PETER
b.1939

GERARDA
b.1939

ALEXANDRA
1901 – 1963

IRMA
1902 – 1986

ALFRED
b.&d.1911

BERTRAM
b.1932

VICTORIA
b.1935

DAGMAR
b.1940

ERNST LEOPOLD
1935 – 1996

CONRADIN
b.1933

CALMA
b.1938

MARIE MELITA
1899 – 1967
=
FRIEDRICH
of Schleswig-Holstein-Glücksburg
1891 – 1965

HANS
1917 – 1944

WILHELM
1919 – 1926

PETER
1922 – 1980

MARIE ALEXANDRA
b.1927

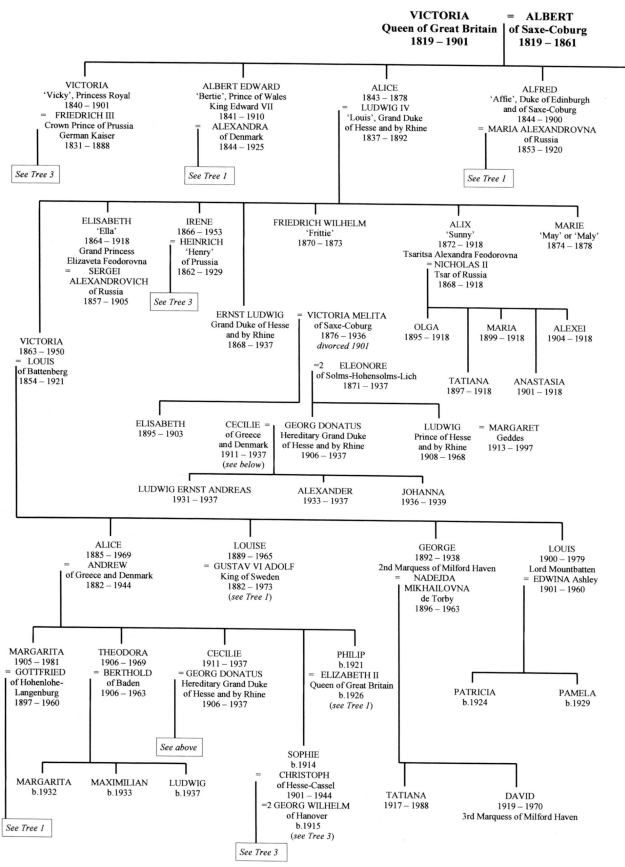

VICTORIA Queen of Great Britain 1819 – 1901 = **ALBERT** of Saxe-Coburg 1819 – 1861

VICTORIA 'Vicky', Princess Royal 1840 – 1901 = **FRIEDRICH III** Crown Prince of Prussia German Kaiser 1831 – 1888

See Tree 3

ALBERT EDWARD 'Bertie', Prince of Wales King Edward VII 1841 – 1910 = **ALEXANDRA** of Denmark 1844 – 1925

See Tree 1

ALICE 1843 – 1878 = **LUDWIG IV** 'Louis', Grand Duke of Hesse and by Rhine 1837 – 1892

ALFRED 'Affie', Duke of Edinburgh and of Saxe-Coburg 1844 – 1900 = **MARIA ALEXANDROVNA** of Russia 1853 – 1920

See Tree 1

ELISABETH 'Ella' 1864 – 1918 Grand Princess Elizaveta Feodorovna = **SERGEI ALEXANDROVICH** of Russia 1857 – 1905

IRENE 1866 – 1953 = **HEINRICH** 'Henry' of Prussia 1862 – 1929

See Tree 3

FRIEDRICH WILHELM 'Frittie' 1870 – 1873

ALIX 'Sunny' 1872 – 1918 Tsaritsa Alexandra Feodorovna = **NICHOLAS II** Tsar of Russia 1868 – 1918

MARIE 'May' or 'Maly' 1874 – 1878

ERNST LUDWIG Grand Duke of Hesse and by Rhine 1868 – 1937 = **VICTORIA MELITA** of Saxe-Coburg 1876 – 1936 *divorced 1901*

=2 **ELEONORE** of Solms-Hohensolms-Lich 1871 – 1937

OLGA 1895 – 1918

TATIANA 1897 – 1918

MARIA 1899 – 1918

ANASTASIA 1901 – 1918

ALEXEI 1904 – 1918

VICTORIA 1863 – 1950 = **LOUIS** of Battenberg 1854 – 1921

ELISABETH 1895 – 1903

CECILIE = of Greece and Denmark 1911 – 1937 *(see below)*

GEORG DONATUS Hereditary Grand Duke of Hesse and by Rhine 1906 – 1937

LUDWIG Prince of Hesse and by Rhine 1908 – 1968 = **MARGARET** Geddes 1913 – 1997

LUDWIG ERNST ANDREAS 1931 – 1937

ALEXANDER 1933 – 1937

JOHANNA 1936 – 1939

ALICE 1885 – 1969 = **ANDREW** of Greece and Denmark 1882 – 1944

LOUISE 1889 – 1965 = **GUSTAV VI ADOLF** King of Sweden 1882 – 1973 *(see Tree 1)*

GEORGE 1892 – 1938 2nd Marquess of Milford Haven = **NADEJDA MIKHAILOVNA** de Torby 1896 – 1963

LOUIS 1900 – 1979 Lord Mountbatten = **EDWINA** Ashley 1901 – 1960

MARGARITA 1905 – 1981 = **GOTTFRIED** of Hohenlohe-Langenburg 1897 – 1960

THEODORA 1906 – 1969 = **BERTHOLD** of Baden 1906 – 1963

CECILIE 1911 – 1937 = **GEORG DONATUS** Hereditary Grand Duke of Hesse and by Rhine 1906 – 1937

See above

PHILIP b.1921 = **ELIZABETH II** Queen of Great Britain b.1926 *(see Tree 1)*

PATRICIA b.1924

PAMELA b.1929

MARGARITA b.1932

MAXIMILIAN b.1933

LUDWIG b.1937

SOPHIE b.1914 = **CHRISTOPH** of Hesse-Cassel 1901 – 1944 =2 **GEORG WILHELM** of Hanover b.1915 *(see Tree 3)*

TATIANA 1917 – 1988

DAVID 1919 – 1970 3rd Marquess of Milford Haven

See Tree 1

See Tree 3

214

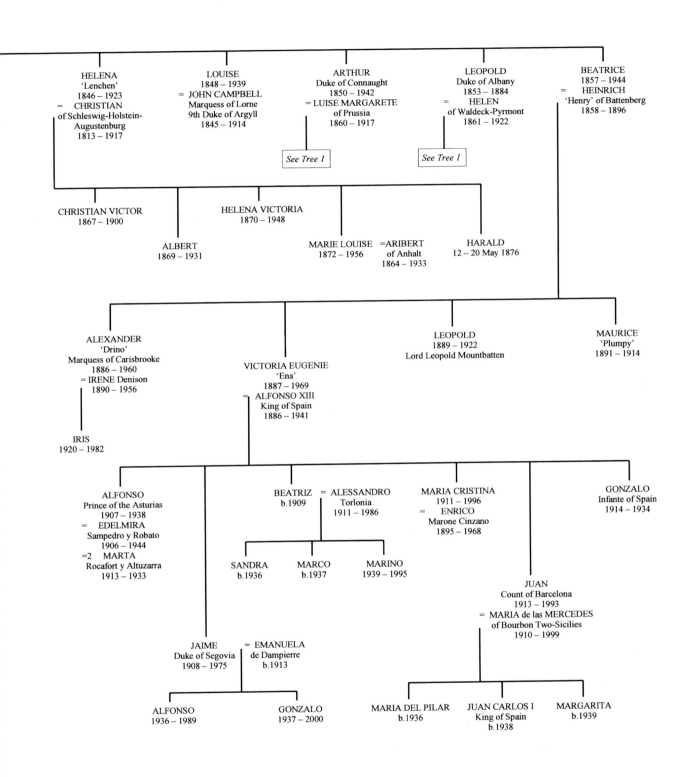

HELENA
'Lenchen'
1846 – 1923
=
CHRISTIAN
of Schleswig-Holstein-
Augustenburg
1813 – 1917

LOUISE
1848 – 1939
= JOHN CAMPBELL
Marquess of Lorne
9th Duke of Argyll
1845 – 1914

ARTHUR
Duke of Connaught
1850 – 1942
= LUISE MARGARETE
of Prussia
1860 – 1917

See Tree 1

LEOPOLD
Duke of Albany
1853 – 1884
=
HELEN
of Waldeck-Pyrmont
1861 – 1922

See Tree 1

BEATRICE
1857 – 1944
=
HEINRICH
'Henry' of Battenberg
1858 – 1896

CHRISTIAN VICTOR
1867 – 1900

ALBERT
1869 – 1931

HELENA VICTORIA
1870 – 1948

MARIE LOUISE
1872 – 1956

=ARIBERT
of Anhalt
1864 – 1933

HARALD
12 – 20 May 1876

ALEXANDER
'Drino'
Marquess of Carisbrooke
1886 – 1960
= IRENE Denison
1890 – 1956

VICTORIA EUGENIE
'Ena'
1887 – 1969
= ALFONSO XIII
King of Spain
1886 – 1941

LEOPOLD
1889 – 1922
Lord Leopold Mountbatten

MAURICE
'Plumpy'
1891 – 1914

IRIS
1920 – 1982

ALFONSO
Prince of the Asturias
1907 – 1938
=
EDELMIRA
Sampedro y Robato
1906 – 1944
=2   MARTA
Rocafort y Altuzarra
1913 – 1933

BEATRIZ
b.1909

= ALESSANDRO
Torlonia
1911 – 1986

MARIA CRISTINA
1911 – 1996
=
ENRICO
Marone Cinzano
1895 – 1968

GONZALO
Infante of Spain
1914 – 1934

SANDRA
b.1936

MARCO
b.1937

MARINO
1939 – 1995

JUAN
Count of Barcelona
1913 – 1993
= MARIA de las MERCEDES
of Bourbon Two-Sicilies
1910 – 1999

JAIME
Duke of Segovia
1908 – 1975

= EMANUELA
de Dampierre
b.1913

ALFONSO
1936 – 1989

GONZALO
1937 – 2000

MARIA DEL PILAR
b.1936

JUAN CARLOS I
King of Spain
b.1938

MARGARITA
b.1939

2: The Families of the Queen's Younger Daughters

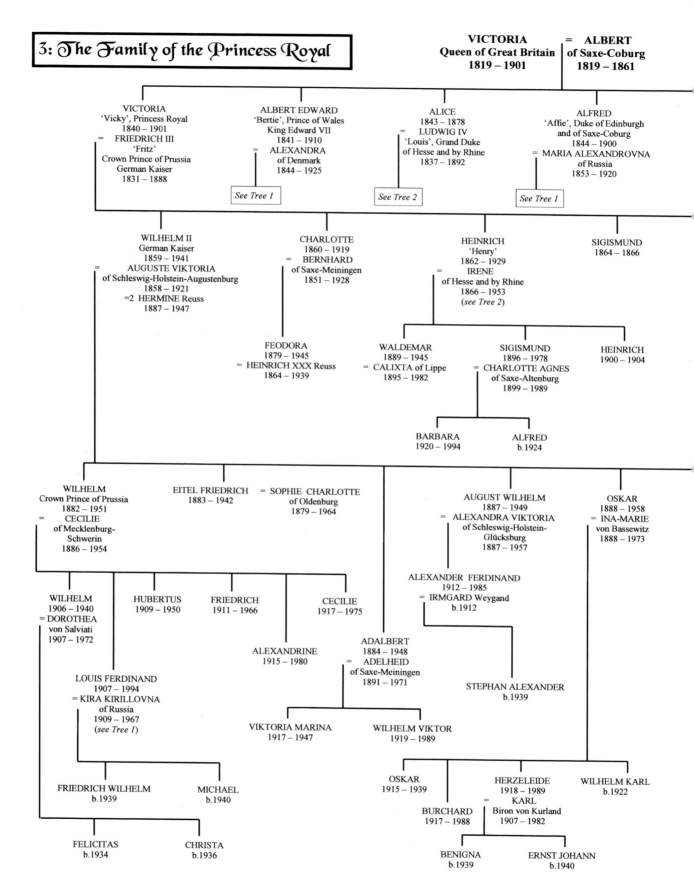

3: The Family of the Princess Royal

VICTORIA
Queen of Great Britain
1819 – 1901
= **ALBERT**
of Saxe-Coburg
1819 – 1861

VICTORIA
'Vicky', Princess Royal
1840 – 1901
= **FRIEDRICH III**
'Fritz'
Crown Prince of Prussia
German Kaiser
1831 – 1888

ALBERT EDWARD
'Bertie', Prince of Wales
King Edward VII
1841 – 1910
= **ALEXANDRA**
of Denmark
1844 – 1925

See Tree 1

ALICE
1843 – 1878
= **LUDWIG IV**
'Louis', Grand Duke
of Hesse and by Rhine
1837 – 1892

See Tree 2

ALFRED
'Affie', Duke of Edinburgh
and of Saxe-Coburg
1844 – 1900
= **MARIA ALEXANDROVNA**
of Russia
1853 – 1920

See Tree 1

WILHELM II
German Kaiser
1859 – 1941
= **AUGUSTE VIKTORIA**
of Schleswig-Holstein-Augustenburg
1858 – 1921
=2 **HERMINE** Reuss
1887 – 1947

CHARLOTTE
1860 – 1919
= **BERNHARD**
of Saxe-Meiningen
1851 – 1928

HEINRICH
'Henry'
1862 – 1929
= **IRENE**
of Hesse and by Rhine
1866 – 1953
(see Tree 2)

SIGISMUND
1864 – 1866

FEODORA
1879 – 1945
= **HEINRICH XXX** Reuss
1864 – 1939

WALDEMAR
1889 – 1945
= **CALIXTA** of Lippe
1895 – 1982

SIGISMUND
1896 – 1978
= **CHARLOTTE AGNES**
of Saxe-Altenburg
1899 – 1989

HEINRICH
1900 – 1904

BARBARA
1920 – 1994

ALFRED
b.1924

WILHELM
Crown Prince of Prussia
1882 – 1951
= **CECILIE**
of Mecklenburg-
Schwerin
1886 – 1954

EITEL FRIEDRICH
1883 – 1942
= **SOPHIE CHARLOTTE**
of Oldenburg
1879 – 1964

AUGUST WILHELM
1887 – 1949
= **ALEXANDRA VIKTORIA**
of Schleswig-Holstein-
Glücksburg
1887 – 1957

OSKAR
1888 – 1958
= **INA-MARIE**
von Bassewitz
1888 – 1973

ALEXANDER FERDINAND
1912 – 1985
= **IRMGARD** Weygand
b.1912

WILHELM
1906 – 1940
= **DOROTHEA**
von Salviati
1907 – 1972

HUBERTUS
1909 – 1950

FRIEDRICH
1911 – 1966

CECILIE
1917 – 1975

ALEXANDRINE
1915 – 1980

ADALBERT
1884 – 1948
= **ADELHEID**
of Saxe-Meiningen
1891 – 1971

STEPHAN ALEXANDER
b.1939

LOUIS FERDINAND
1907 – 1994
= **KIRA KIRILLOVNA**
of Russia
1909 – 1967
(see Tree 1)

VIKTORIA MARINA
1917 – 1947

WILHELM VIKTOR
1919 – 1989

FRIEDRICH WILHELM
b.1939

MICHAEL
b.1940

OSKAR
1915 – 1939

HERZELEIDE
1918 – 1989
= **KARL**
Biron von Kurland
1907 – 1982

WILHELM KARL
b.1922

BURCHARD
1917 – 1988

FELICITAS
b.1934

CHRISTA
b.1936

BENIGNA
b.1939

ERNST JOHANN
b.1940

216

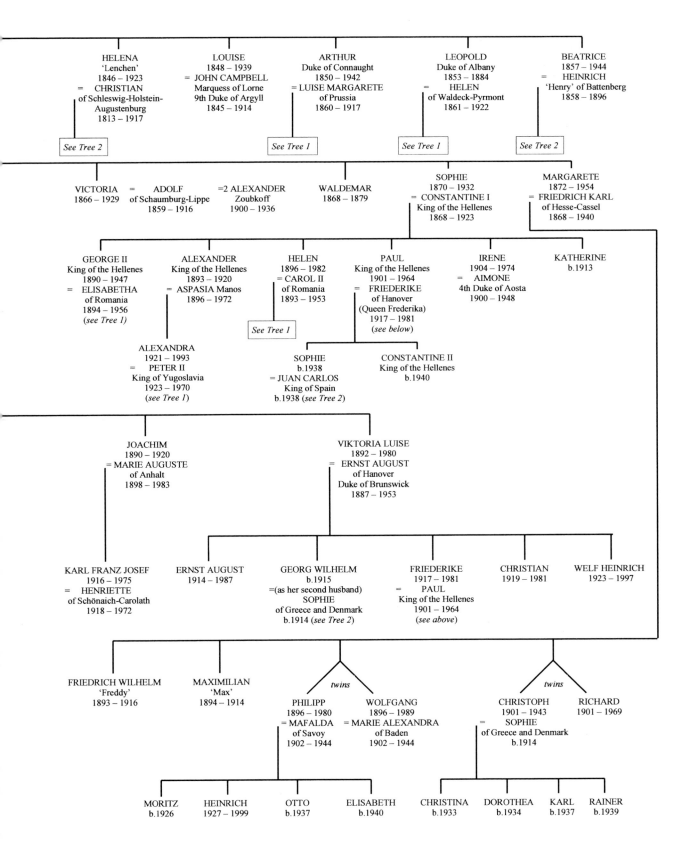

HELENA
'Lenchen'
1846 – 1923
=
CHRISTIAN
of Schleswig-Holstein-
Augustenburg
1813 – 1917

See Tree 2

LOUISE
1848 – 1939
= JOHN CAMPBELL
Marquess of Lorne
9th Duke of Argyll
1845 – 1914

See Tree 1

ARTHUR
Duke of Connaught
1850 – 1942
= LUISE MARGARETE
of Prussia
1860 – 1917

LEOPOLD
Duke of Albany
1853 – 1884
=
HELEN
of Waldeck-Pyrmont
1861 – 1922

See Tree 1

BEATRICE
1857 – 1944
=
HEINRICH
'Henry' of Battenberg
1858 – 1896

See Tree 2

VICTORIA
1866 – 1929
= ADOLF
of Schaumburg-Lippe
1859 – 1916

=2 ALEXANDER
Zoubkoff
1900 – 1936

WALDEMAR
1868 – 1879

SOPHIE
1870 – 1932
= CONSTANTINE I
King of the Hellenes
1868 – 1923

MARGARETE
1872 – 1954
= FRIEDRICH KARL
of Hesse-Cassel
1868 – 1940

GEORGE II
King of the Hellenes
1890 – 1947
=
ELISABETHA
of Romania
1894 – 1956
(see Tree 1)

ALEXANDER
King of the Hellenes
1893 – 1920
= ASPASIA Manos
1896 – 1972

HELEN
1896 – 1982
= CAROL II
of Romania
1893 – 1953

See Tree 1

PAUL
King of the Hellenes
1901 – 1964
=
FRIEDERIKE
of Hanover
(Queen Frederika)
1917 – 1981
(see below)

IRENE
1904 – 1974
=
AIMONE
4th Duke of Aosta
1900 – 1948

KATHERINE
b.1913

ALEXANDRA
1921 – 1993
=
PETER II
King of Yugoslavia
1923 – 1970
(see Tree 1)

SOPHIE
b.1938
= JUAN CARLOS
King of Spain
b.1938 (see Tree 2)

CONSTANTINE II
King of the Hellenes
b.1940

JOACHIM
1890 – 1920
= MARIE AUGUSTE
of Anhalt
1898 – 1983

VIKTORIA LUISE
1892 – 1980
=
ERNST AUGUST
of Hanover
Duke of Brunswick
1887 – 1953

KARL FRANZ JOSEF
1916 – 1975
=
HENRIETTE
of Schönaich-Carolath
1918 – 1972

ERNST AUGUST
1914 – 1987

GEORG WILHELM
b.1915
=(as her second husband)
SOPHIE
of Greece and Denmark
b.1914 (see Tree 2)

FRIEDERIKE
1917 – 1981
=
PAUL
King of the Hellenes
1901 – 1964
(see above)

CHRISTIAN
1919 – 1981

WELF HEINRICH
1923 – 1997

FRIEDRICH WILHELM
'Freddy'
1893 – 1916

MAXIMILIAN
'Max'
1894 – 1914

twins

PHILIPP
1896 – 1980
= MAFALDA
of Savoy
1902 – 1944

WOLFGANG
1896 – 1989
= MARIE ALEXANDRA
of Baden
1902 – 1944

twins

CHRISTOPH
1901 – 1943
=
SOPHIE
of Greece and Denmark
b.1914

RICHARD
1901 – 1969

MORITZ
b.1926

HEINRICH
1927 – 1999

OTTO
b.1937

ELISABETH
b.1940

CHRISTINA
b.1933

DOROTHEA
b.1934

KARL
b.1937

RAINER
b.1939

Notes

The most helpful reference book on Queen Victoria's family is Marlene A. Eilers, *Queen Victoria's Descendants* [Rosvall Royal Books, Falköping, Sweden, 1997]

Ronald Allison & Sarah Riddell (eds.), *The Royal Encyclopedia* [Macmillan 1991] contains a wealth of information.

On photography and the royal family Frances Dimond and Roger Taylor's *Crown & Camera; the royal family and photography 1842–1910* is invaluable.

SPECIFIC SOURCES

Introduction

p. x   'I have been writing ... for a Photograph!', Mrs Steuart Erskine (ed.), *Twenty Years at Court* [Nisbet 1916], p. 377

p. x   'You must send me the bill . . .', Charlotte Zeepvat, *Prince Leopold* [Sutton Publishing 1998], p. 68

Chapter 1

p. 2   'He is the oddest ... photographer', quoted by Helmut Gernsheim in *Happy and Glorious; 130 Years of Royal Photographs* [National Portrait Gallery 1977], p. 26

p. 2   'We have been amusing ... less interesting', *Twenty Years at Court*, p. 289

p. 4   'Prince of Wales is improved ... not at all obstinate', *Twenty Years*, p. 364

p. 5   'Prince Alfred ... aware of the fact', *Twenty Years*, p. 368

p. 5   'Lenchen's features . . .', Queen Victoria to the Princess Royal, from Roger Fulford (ed.), *Dearest Child* [Evans 1964], p. 175

p. 7   'with little pieces of poetry ... a little naughty', *Twenty Years*, p. 371

p. 10   'I never saw anything so pretty . . .', *Twenty Years*, p. 250

p. 16   'This child is dear . . .', Mary Howard McClintock, *The Queen Thanks Sir Howard* [John Murray 1945], p. 25

Chapter 2

p. 23   'Princess Alice and her Louis ... deciding for her', *Twenty Years*, p. 379

p. 24   'God knows ... we do not', *Dearest Child*, p. 223

Chapter 3

p. 37   'very odd ... very frequently', Roger Fulford (ed.), *Your Dear Letter* [Evans 1971], p. 114

p. 37   'cries and grumbles . . .', *Your Dear Letter*, p. 36

p. 39   'Ella, who was breakfasting ... tractable child', HRH Princess Alice, *Letters to Her Majesty The Queen* [John Murray 1897], p. 151

p. 40   'What a nice ... the photograph', *Your Dear Letter*, p. 168

p. 41   'I fear ... Windsor Park', *Your Dear Letter*, pp. 200–1

p. 42   'My first impression ... fond of immediately', T. Herbert Warren, *Christian Victor; the Story of a Young Soldier* [John Murray 1903], pp. 10–11

p. 42   'a very clever, sharp boy ... I laughed heartily', *Christian Victor*, p. 18

p. 43   'Ella is another child ... God's will be done', *Letters to Her Majesty The Queen*, p. 237

p. 44   'It is very good ... greedy', Roger Fulford (ed.), *Darling Child* [Evans 1976], p. 163

p. 47   'She was so nice ... beautiful woman', Grand Duke Ernst Ludwig of Hesse and by Rhine, *Erinnertes* [Eduard Roether, Darmstadt, 1983], p. 88

p. 49   'a great darling . . .', Richard Hough (ed.), *Advice to a Granddaughter* [Heinemann 1975], p. 36

p. 50   'The baby ... afraid of the imp', Hampshire CRO 39M85/PCF30; Dr G.V. Poore to his mother, 19 November 1883

p. 53   'Drino & Ena ... so strong', James Pope-Hennessy (ed.), *Queen Victoria at Windsor and Balmoral* [George Allen and Unwin 1959], p. 37

Chapter 4

p. 61   'I can't tell you ... anything to do with it', Roger Fulford (ed.), *Beloved Mama* [Evans 1981], p. 110

Acknowledgements

The Royal Archives © H.M. Queen Elizabeth II: 9, 10 [both], 20, 56[top]
© Staatsarchiv Darmstadt; 127[top]
Nancy Tryon Collection; 72, 114[top], 141, 174[top], 179, 181[bottom], 202[both]
John Wimbles Collection; 108[bottom], 116[top], 119

All other photographs in this book are from the private collections of the author and friends: my special thanks go out to Frances Dimond and Helen Gray of the Royal Photographic Collection at Windsor, to Dr E.G. Franz of the Staatsarchiv Darmstadt, to Harold Brown, Nancy Tryon, John Wimbles, Arthur Addington, John Eagle, David Cripps, Alan Stubbs, Helen Berger, Sue Woolmans and David Horbury for helping to find and identify photographs, for lending photographs, for helping with information and for showing an interest in the project – and not forgetting my agent, Sheila Watson, my editors Jaqueline Mitchell and Clare Bishop and my mother, because my collection is also her collection.

Every effort has been made to trace and contact the original owners of all photographs. If copyright has inadvertently been infringed, copyright holders should write to the publisher with full details. Upon copyright being established, a correct credit will be incorporated into future editions of the book.

The work of the following photographers is represented:

Abels, 210
Afanasjev, S., 173[top]
Anthony, Ypres, 164[bottom]
Aune, Norway, 111[top]
Backofen, Darmstadt, 47[top]
Bambridge, 11[bottom]
Bassano/Rotary, 156
Bergamasco, St Petersburg, 30[top]
Berger, G., Potsdam, 62[top]
Bettini, Rome, 198
Bingham, 12[top]
Blau, Ursula, Potsdam, 187, 195
Boasch, Walter, Eckernforde, 168
Boissonas & Eggler, 128[bottom], 135
Boucas, Geo., Athens, 70[bottom],
    144[bottom], 162[top], 171[both], 200[top]

Brockmeyer, Luise, Darmstadt, 181[top],
    182[both], 184[both], 185, 202[top], 203
Brodrene, Halversen, Norway, 189[bottom]
Byrne, Richmond, 52[top], 62[top]
Caldesi, 10[bottom]
Carrell, Ghitta, Rome, 183[top]
Central News, 158[bottom]
Charles, Lallie, 144[top]
Corbett, Alexander, 174[bottom], 175[bottom],
    177[top]
Dänzer, Coburg, 180[bottom]
Deane & Martin, Brighton, 124[bottom]
Disderi, Paris, 22[bottom]
Downey, W. & D., ix, 12[bottom], 18[top], 29,
    30[bottom], 39[both], 46, 54[bottom],
    59[bottom], 74, 89[bottom], 90[bottom],

The remainder are unidentified in the original.

Index

Page numbers in italic refer to illustrations